Jubilee

Peter Barnes

Methuen Drama

Published by Methuen 2001

1 3 5 7 9 10 8 6 4 2

First published in 2001 by
Methuen Publishing Limited, 215 Vauxhall Bridge Road,
London SW1V 1EJ

Methuen Publishing Limited Reg. No. 3543167

A CIP catalogue record for this book is available from the British Library.

ISBN 0 413 76130 4

Typeset by SX Composing DTP, Rayleigh, Essex
Printed and bound in Great Britain by
Cox & Wyman Ltd, Reading, Berkshire

Jubilee

Peter Barnes is a writer and director, and one of Britain's
most controversial dramatists, repeatedly challenging the
parameters of theatrical convention. His plays are
distinguished by their biting satire and anarchic mix of
comedy and tragedy. His work includes *The Ruling Class*
(Nottingham and Piccadilly Theatre, London, 1968),
Leonardo's Last Supper and *Noonday Demons* (Open Space
Theatre, London, 1969), *The Bewitched* (RSC, Aldwych
Theatre, London, 1974), *Laughter!* (Royal Court Theatre,
1978), *Red Noses* (RSC, Barbican, 1985) and *Sunsets and Glories*
(West Yorkshire Playhouse, Leeds, 1990). He has won the
Evening Standard Award and the John Whiting Award,
1969; Sony Best Play Award, 1981; Laurence Olivier Award,
1985; Royal Television Society Award for Best TV Play,
1987; and was nominated for an Oscar in 1993.

for
Leela

Jubilee premiered at the Swan Theatre, Stratford, on 12 July 2001. The cast was as follows (in order of appearance):

Ben Jonson / William Hunt	Geoffrey Freshwater
William Shakespeare /	
Charles Macklin /	
George Steevens	Paul Bentall
John Ange	David Hinton
Thomas Sharp / James Boswell	Owen Sharpe
Rev. Francis Gastrell /	
Dr Thomas Arne	Michael Mears
Francis Wheeler	James Telfer
Reverand Jago	Trevor Martin
David Garrick	Nicholas Woodeson
Jack Grimes	Stephen Noonan
Eva Maria Garrick	Kelly Hunter
George Garrick	David Collings
Samuel Johnson / Lord Dorset	Barry Stanton
Nell /Lydia	Amanda Drew
Amos Ackers	Mark Hadfield
Ted Ackers	Wayne Cater
Mrs Ross	Carol Macready
Hermione	Angela Vale
Charmaine	Elizabeth Hurran
Charles Dibdin	Joseph England
Jimmy	Jack Gayler /Callum Finlay
Bill	Joshua Vizor / Callum Roberts
Jack	James Hoyle / Paul Rothwell
John Payton	Drew Mulligan

The **Peddlers, Wigmakers, Wardrobe Mistress, Stage Manager, Assistant Stage Manager, Jubilee Guests, Chefs** and **Chorus** were played by members of the company.

Directed by Gregory Doran
Designed by Robert Jones
Lighting by Tim Mitchell
Music by Stephen Deutsch
Movement by Sian Williams
Sound by Martin Slavin
Fight Directing by Terry King

Act One

Prologue

1608 Stratford upon Avon. A single mulberry tree, downstage right. Two old writers, **Ben Jonson** *and* **William Shakespeare**, *sit under it, drinking ale in the autumn sunlight.*

Jonson
Shakespeare } (*singing*) 'Swan, swan, swim over the sea / Swim swan, for me / Swim swan, swim / Swan in the rain / Swim back again / I'd like to see / You swim swan just swim for me / Swim swan, swim.'

Shakespeare   'To be or not to be alive . . .'

Jonson   That's wrong, Bill.

Shakespeare   I've forgotten every line I ever wrote, Ben.

Jonson   They earned you a pretty penny and a few ugly ones.

Shakespeare   Should've been more! Those ferret-eyed, cow-hearted theatre owners sliced off more than their share.

Jonson   You were one yourself.

Shakespeare   That's different. They only let me gouge the odd stray guinea. Cheats! Cheats!

Jonson   They can't trust their arses with a fart, but they can rob poor artists blind.

Shakespeare   Those cribbage creepers will always be with us, Ben, like vomit and death.

Jonson   'Vomit and death.' I'll use it, William, I'm still writing.

Shakespeare   Why? When you can be in fresh grass, with a corn stalk between your teeth, gawking up at clouds. Retire, Ben, retire.

Jonson   Into what damp ditch? Look at my tights! They don't follow the contours of my leg like they should. I'll never be able to retire and afford tights sculptured to the wearer's special requirements like yours.

Shakespeare   I was going mad, of course . . . 'I wish mine eyes would with themselves shut up my thoughts' . . . that told me I was done. Time to enjoy my ill-gotten gains, Ben. You still haven't thrown away the bloody quill. I've never understood you. You're the cleverest man I know, but you were seduced by art.

Jonson   At an early age.

Shakespeare   I wrote for money and when I had enough I stopped.

Jonson   I wrote to change the world.

Shakespeare   It needs obliterating, not changing.

Jonson   I wanted my work to endure, so I wrote for future generations.

Shakespeare   What've future generations ever done for you? There's no profit in living and dying poor, to delight future fools. Even if there was profit, you wouldn't be able to enjoy it, you'd be dead. Let the future rot like we'll soon rot. It doesn't deserve us.

Jonson   Of course it doesn't. The future's fickle. They'll consign the best to oblivion and praise the worst for the wrong reasons. But I still believe I had something to say to them.

Shakespeare   I had something to say too . . . 'Give me the money, fart-heads!' They don't care about us so why should we care about them? Audiences, past, present and future, high or low, I spit on them all!

Jonson   But in secret, eh, William? You kowtowed to the mighty with the best of us.

Shakespeare   That's where the money is. I crept and crawled, flattened and flattered, like any palm-itching politician. My plays're full of respect for authority – it's where the gold's buried – and full of contempt for ordinary folk who have only empty pockets. That's why my work was so popular. English servility has no bottom. You were always too radical, Ben.

Jonson   I'm paying for it now. I'll die poor, William.

Shakespeare   So how goes London?

Jonson   Vile.

Shakespeare   Viler here. The country's flat and the people flatter. Nothing worse than money-grubbing rustics.

Jonson   Why live here?

Shakespeare   It's home.

As they drink, **Peter Barnes** *creeps in stage right, with a chair, and sits near them.*

Barnes   I hope you don't mind?

Shakespeare   We do, this is private property . . . this land, this ale, this mulberry tree. I bought 'em all, stamped W. Shakespeare Esquire, so I don't have to share 'em with louse-ridden strangers like you.

Barnes   Let me introduce myself, Peter Barnes.

Shakespeare   Do you know him, Ben? No . . . so leave, sir, before I call the constable!

Jonson   Go, squire, vanish! This isn't your place.

Barnes   No, it's my dream.

Jonson   Your dream? . . . this is a dream? . . . That doesn't mean we have to share our ale with you, does it?

Barnes   Not unless you want to.

Shakespeare
Jonson } We don't!

Shakespeare   Why're you dreaming us?

Barnes   Because I'm writing a play about Shakespeare.

Jonson   Why?

Barnes   I'm being paid to.

Shakespeare   Otherwise you wouldn't?

Barnes   Never.

Shakespeare   You're a true writer, sir! . . . give that man a drink!

Jonson *hands* **Barnes** *a tankard of ale.*

Barnes   It isn't actually about you, more about David Garrick. There's probably an anniversary coming up soon. The English're big on anniversaries, they have nothing much to look forward to, so they look back. The Stratford Theatre want to commemorate the first celebration of your birth put on by an eighteenth-century actor, David Garrick. It's an excuse for them to make more money selling cheap Shakespearean knick-knacks.

Shakespeare   Why did they pick you?

Barnes   Desperate.

Jonson   How's the piece going?

Barnes   Hard to say, I'm only on the prologue.

Shakespeare   So they still remember my work? I thought the only thing that would outlast me would be that mulberry tree.

Barnes   Your work's revered.

Jonson   And me?

Barnes   Scholars, mostly.

Jonson   Oh, Lord . . . So we pant for fame and glory /
Deeming fame and glory all / Though we know how wide
the earth is / And our claims of fame so small. / Even if our
quick-swelling glory / Would hardly fill a narrow room, /
Still we strive however vainly / To escape our doom. /
Then at last we see life's bitter shortness / Lengthened by
fame's mortal breath / But there waits for us, when it is
taken / A second death.

Shakespeare   Ben, you should've concentrated on kings,
queens and princes. It pays to be a snob . . . all that stuff about
ordinary people doesn't play in England, green and pleasant.

Jonson   But I was *funny*!

Shakespeare   So was I.

Jonson   Only because you had that clown, William
Kemp, in your company.

Shakespeare   Last seen morris dancing across the Alps!

Jonson *and* **Shakespeare** *morris dance on the spot before
slumping down in their chairs, roaring with laughter.*

Shakespeare   It just shows the future has no taste. We were
all hacks; pen-pushing stinkards trying to earn a living . . . me,
Kit Marlow, Johnny Marston, Tommy Middleton and the rest.

Jonson   Ten-a-penny rhymesters.

Shakespeare   I've told you before, Ben, don't suffer for
your art, it won't suffer for you! It doesn't matter what
esteem my work's held in, I can't receive a half groat extra
for it now. Others profit, not me. So what does it matter,
fame or oblivion? We ghosts can't enjoy any of it. What's
Hamlet to me or the *Iliad* to poor blind Homer?

Jonson   I always admired you, William, for getting out
when you were still in the black.

Shakespeare   Henry did even better.

Jonson   Never stopped writing.

Shakespeare   Must've made a fortune.

Barnes   Henry who?

Jonson   Henry . . . Henry.

Shakespeare   Henry Chettle . . . a giant.

Barnes   I've never heard of him.

Jonson   You don't know Henry Chettle? Wrote over fifty plays . . . some were even good.

Barnes   Forgotten, now.

Shakespeare   That gives you some idea of the taste of future generations. Henry Chettle made more money out of playwriting than any of us. You can't go against that. It's the only objective critical standard that makes sense. The rest is just white wine with fish . . . purely personal.

Barnes   I didn't go to sleep to dream of Henry Chettle.

Jonson   You could do worse . . . good man, Chettle.

Barnes   I'm surprised you agree with these sentiments, Mr Jonson.

Jonson   I came round to them in time as a sensible man must. Of course, sometimes we didn't write just for money . . . there was poetry.

Shakespeare   We all wrote it. But that was mainly to ingratiate ourselves with various piss-stinkin' princes.

Jonson   I learnt one painful lesson from hard years chained to desk and pen, a well-turned line never stopped a brute from beating your brains out.

Barnes   And our best work will never get produced.

Jonson   I still have the blistering comedy, *The Whorehouse Whoremaster*, mouldering in a cupboard somewhere. Can't even get the rats to look at it. It's being nibbled to pieces by *mice*!

Shakespeare   So you're going to celebrate my birth? . . .
What did I do to deserve it?

Jonson   What did *we* do?

Barnes   You provided work for an army of academics.
Without you they'd be unemployable.

Jonson   But we didn't change anything! Not in our time,
your time, and in no time at all we came to dust.

Shakespeare   The wicked keep living. The older they are
the richer they get. Their families increase. They're safe,
they don't have to be afraid of the likes of us.

Jonson   They sing and dance, and live well and go down
to their graves in peace. How often are their lamps blown
out before their time? How often are they punished?

Shakespeare   Never. Priests say God punishes a man's
children for his sins – cow-turds! Let God punish the man
himself. What does the mouldering corpse care about the
evil he leaves behind?

Jonson   They tell you that tyrants and oppressors are
spared for the day God judges them . . . too late! Who
speaks against them for the way they acted?

Shakespeare   Who pays them back for what they've
done? Not us.

Barnes   I didn't think you'd be so bitter.

Shakespeare   It's your dream, not ours.

Jonson *and* **Shakespeare** *rise and sing a new, sad arrangement
of 'Here We Go Round The Mulberry Bush'.* **Barnes** *gets up and
sings with them in close harmony.*

Lights out.

Scene One

The song is replaced by loud 'chopping' and a cry of 'TIMBER!', followed by the sound of a tree crashing to the ground. Lights up on the same garden, 1756. The mulberry tree, now much larger, has just been cut down by **John Ange***, who continues swinging his axe and chopping branches off the tree whilst the* **Reverend Francis Gastrell** *trembles and covers his face with his hands.*

Ange   It's done, Reverend. Too late for weeping.

Rev. Gastrell   I'm not weeping, I'm laughing.

Ange   That's laughing?

Rev. Gastrell   I don't laugh much so I'm out of practice. I'm laughing in relief, Master Ange. Mark the date, August the seventh, seventeen fifty-six. That tree's plagued me for years, now it's down and out!

Ange   No way to put it back, that's for sure.

Rev. Gastrell   I bought this house so I could spend my summers in peace and tranquillity. After the terrible pressures of being Vicar of Frodsham and Canon Residentrary at Lichfield, I just wanted to rest and do nothing.

Ange   Stratford's the place for doing nothing.

Rev. Gastrell   So I thought. But that damnable tree's made my life hell here . . . keep chopping, Mr Ange, keep chopping.

Ange   Isn't it the tree Master Shakespeare planted?

Rev. Gastrell   Every day I've had goggle-eyed visitors at my door asking to see it . . . chop-chop, Mr Ange, chop-chop . . . they disturb the household, ask me questions about a scribbler I don't know from Adam. Why should I? He's no relation of mine.

Ange   They say he was good, in his way.

Rev. Gastrell It depends who you talk to . . . but it's why so many of the visitors are actor chappies . . . horrible! Horrible!

Ange I've seen 'em tramping over your flowerbeds, Reverend.

Rev. Gastrell Louts! Misshappen hell-spawn! . . . And they send small boys back to steal twigs and wormy bark . . . there's one now! . . . I see you, sir!

He picks up a rock and flings it at someone in the wings stage right. There is a yell of pain as the rock finds its mark. **Thomas Sharp** *hurries in stage left.*

Sharp Sharp by name, sharp by nature . . . let's talk money.

Rev. Gastrell Blessèd is he that cometh in the name of gold and silver.

Ange (*chopping*) Money! . . . Money!

Sharp It is the supreme good. Therefore the man who possesses it is good . . . money saves us the trouble of being dishonest.

Ange (*chopping*) Money! . . . Money!

Rev. Gastrell I'm stupid but I have money. But how can a man with money be stupid?

Sharp Money converts all our weaknesses into strengths. It transforms hate into love, love into hate, vice into virtue, and vice versa. It is the true creative force in the Universe.

Ange (*chopping*) Money! . . . Money!

Rev. Gastrell With money I can achieve all the human heart longs for.

Ange
Rev. Gastrell } MONEY! . . . MONEY!
Sharp

Sharp   Reverend Gastrell, I wish to purchase that wood
. . . shall we say one guinea?

Rev. Gastrell   That's generous, Mr Sharp. Too generous
for a pile of firewood.

Sharp   I've nothing to hide. With Master Ange's help, I
mean to carve shapely Shakespearean boxes, rings and
other knick-knackeries from it and to sell them to summer
visitors who can no longer see the tree Shakespeare planted.

Rev. Gastrell   I suppose there'll be enough deluded fools
who'll pay. I don't need the wood but you do, that means
it'll cost you *two* guineas, sir!

Sharp *gives him two gold coins.*

Sharp   That's mighty expensive for such a small pile of
wood but I'm counting on the cult of the blessèd William to
grow as fast as that pile. His followers meet every
Wednesday to drink, recite his verse and worship at his
grave.

Rev. Gastrell   It's blasphemous. Luckily I won't be here
to see it. I've decided to leave and find better summer
accommodation.

Ange   A wise move, Reverend. Your neighbours won't like
you a-chopping down this tree.

Rev. Gastrell   Sentimental hogwash!

Ange   No, it's money again and there's never anything
sentimental about money. Visitors paid good coin to tavern
keepers to drink where they think the blessèd William drank
and visit the tree he sat under.

There is the sound of an angry mob and glass breaking upstage centre.

Sharp   It's the wild burghers of Stratford on the rampage.

Ange   They've heard about the tree.

The **Rev. Gastrell** *whips out two pistols.*

Rev. Gastrell   Stratford rabble!

He runs off stage left firing his pistols. There is the sound of the mob stampeding away.

Sharp   Now we can get down to business.

Ange   Half this tree is dead wood, sir, rotten from within. I reckon the good stuff'll provide us with less than a year's work.

A huge backdrop of wooden planks falls upstage with a crash. It stretches like a wall across the stage and up to the flies.

Sharp   More mulberry wood!

Ange   That's not mulberry.

Sharp   *We* know that but we're experts . . . buyers won't know the difference. For them it's Shakespeare's own mulberry tree. There's enough wood here to make thousands of Shakespearean knick-knackeries. Like splinters from Christ's True Cross, we have an inexhaustible supply.

Ange   Is it honest?

Sharp   What's that? In our own way we're spreading the good word about brother William. Shakespeare needs us. We're his first disciples, sowing the seeds of the true faith.

Lights down on them upstage as three Stratford dignitaries, **William Hunt**, **Francis Wheeler** *and the aged* **Reverend Jago** *enter chanting, downstage left.*

Wheeler ⎫ 'Oh, Willy, Oh, Willy, save the town / Let
Hunt   ⎬ them dote / On what you wrote / So long as
Rev. Jago ⎭ they spend / We'll be your best friend /
Proclaim your name / Build up your fame / Oh, Willy, Oh, Willy, hear our call / And save us all.

Wheeler   It's decided, then, David Garrick, actor extraordinaire, is our man.

Hunt   We'll ask him to open the new Town Hall, dedicate a bust of William Shakespeare and stage a one-day Jubilee in honour of the Bard. Do you think he'll do it?

Rev. Jago   We're offering him the freedom of Stratford. What more can he want?

Wheeler   Money?

Hunt   He must do it for the honour and for love of Shakespeare.

Rev. Jago   Like we all are, with no thought of mercenary gain.

They nod as the lights fade down and **Peddlers** *rush on, selling cheap wooden knick-knacks from trays. Their cries echo all around in the dark.*

Peddlers' Voices   Boxes, keyring, lovingly carved from Shakespeare's own mulberry tree! . . . Buy! . . . arty artefacts . . . own part of a great artist! . . . Buy! . . . Special offer . . . the Bard of Stratford-upon-Avon . . . the world's leading poet! . . . A likeness! . . . Buy! . . . Buy! . . . Buy!

Scene Two

Garrick*'s small dressing room, Covent Garden Theatre.* **Garrick** *is being dressed for the night's performance of* Richard III *by his dresser,* **Jack Grimes***, whilst* **Garrick***'s wife,* **Eva Maria***, practises dance steps.*

Garrick   I'm tempted by the offer of staging a Stratford Jubilee.

Mrs Garrick   Let someone else do it. You're tired, you've had a long season. We should go somewhere quiet, where the days seem like weeks, the weeks like months and the months like years.

Garrick   I've been to Bournemouth . . . why won't you stay still?

Mrs Garrick   I'm a dancer.

Garrick   You don't have to dance to prove it.

Mrs Garrick   How else will they know?

Garrick   Tell them.

Mrs Garrick   People lie, just like the fat burghers of Stratford lie when they say they care for Shakespeare. Why would, should, or could they care for a poet? They're only interested in putting that Stratford on the map.

Grimes   Sure, but they're all up to their armpits in pig shit. Steer clear of 'em, Davey darlin', or as sure as Connemara eggs're eggs, you'll regret it.

Garrick   Begorra and begore, sure but I'll not listen to the demented ravings of a Stage Irishman.

Grimes   No one calls Milo O'Casey a Stage Irishman!

Garrick   Of course not . . . your name's Jack Grimes.

Grimes   Alias Donald Teagarden, late of the Northampton Players . . . listen to your old mucker and mate, Davey. They're a bunch of Stratford crab-faced coney-men, and crooks.

Garrick   Hmm, if anyone should know, you should, Jack.

George Garrick *hurries in, sneezing.*

Mrs Garrick   You look ill, George.

George Garrick   If I felt that good I'd be happy. Delegation from Stratford to see you, brother.

Garrick   Show 'em out, George!

George Garrick   They haven't been shown in yet . . . gentlemen, Mr David Garrick.

Wheeler, Hunt and **Rev. Jago** *come in. Despite the fact that the small dressing room is now jammed with seven people,* **Mrs Garrick** *still tries to dance.*

Rev. Jago   Sir, an honour, sir . . . the world needs compassion, sir, don't you agree? This is Mr Hunt and Mr Wheeler and I am . . . who am I? . . . no, no, don't tell me, let me guess . . . the Reverend James Jago! . . . That's an easy name to remember.

George Garrick   Out gentlemen!

Garrick   No, no, my brother's overworked and underpaid . . . it's an honour to meet you, this is my wife, Eva Maria . . . and my dresser, Jack Grimes, alias Milo O'Casey, formerly Donald Teagarden, actor, comic and champion Irish clog dancer.

Grimes   Bless this house and good morrow to yous all.

Hunt   You played Launcelot Gobbo . . . marvellous!

Grimes   Never did but if I had it would've been marvellous!

Wheeler   Mr Garrick, we're here to find out if you've decided to head our one-day Jubilee?

Hunt   And dedicate a bust of the divine William in the magnificent new Stratford Town Hall. We'd heard you've a temple to the Bard in your garden.

Charles Macklin, *another leading actor, strides in.*

Macklin   Davey, laddie! . . . Eva, m' darlin'.

He kisses **Mrs Garrick**.

Garrick   Gentlemen, this is Charles Macklin.

Macklin   No applause while I'm drinking . . . Grimes, get me a tankard, you Irish toss-pot! . . . You see before you the wreck of a man. I've spent a split week in Barnsley . . . what further humiliations're in store, I ask the uncomprehending heavens? We opened last Wednesday. It should've been Good Friday, the way I was crucified. The stars're retrograde, Davey. There's nothing I can do. Down, down, down goes Macklin . . . Davey, I've come to congratulate you on last night's performance. It was . . . how shall I put it?

George Garrick   Put it somewhere or it'll go off.

Grimes *hands* **Macklin** *a bottle of beer.*

Garrick   'Overwhelming'.

Macklin   'Overwhelming' is the word . . . what're you overwhelming tonight?

Garrick   *Richard III* . . . ahh! . . . Where's my hump?! . . . My hump!

Grimes   I've got it.

With great difficulty, because the room is jammed with people, he starts to strap the hump on to **Garrick**'s *back.*

Mrs Garrick   We're all getting the hump, my sweet.

Macklin   Why is it so crowded in here?

Wheeler   We're trying to persuade Mr Garrick to open our first Shakespeare Jubilee in Stratford.

Macklin   Why didn't you ask me?

Rev. Jago   Who're you, sir, if that's not an idle question? And even if it is, I don't care. I speak my mind.

Macklin   Charles Macklin, sir! I once bestrode the town's boards as friend Davey bestrides 'em now. Every word, every gesture was admired, talked of and greeted with applause. I was fashionable. Then, little by little, it happened. I didn't notice it till it was too late. Those words, those gestures, so lately adored, were now greeted with disdain and silence. I had become unfashionable.

Wheeler   You were an actor?

Macklin   Ah, you have a discerning eye for the obvious.

Grimes   You should've seen his *Richard II*. With much ado, he was the Jew that Shakespeare drew. I saw it under unfortunate conditions . . . the seats were facing the stage.

Macklin   I saw your act once, Grimes. The audience's eyes kept wandering to the reassuring notice at the top of the programme . . . 'If needed, this theatre can be emptied in three minutes. Choose the nearest exit to your seat and try not to run.'

Wheeler   I never go to the theatre.

Macklin   So why're you holding a Shakespeare Jubilee?

Wheeler   Money.

Hunt   It's Mr Wheeler's little joke. That's what makes us different. I've no sense of humour . . . the reason for the Jubilee is we consider Shakespeare a British treasure and wish to promote him to a permanent place in the national conscience.

Garrick   And Stratford-upon-Avon with him?

Rev. Jago   Naturally. It goes without saying, so I'm saying it.

The **Assistant Stage Manager** *comes in with a tray of food.*

Garrick   Ah, cucumber sandwiches, and smoked ham . . . no fat, no fat!

The **Asst** *squeezes his way across the packed room as two female* **Wigmakers** *come in.*

First Wigmaker   Your new wig, Master G!

Garrick   I trust it's not like the last one . . . it slid off my head in a high wind and was lost under the wheels of a coach headed for Dungeness . . . everyone breathe in!

There is an audible gasp as everyone breathes in, and the two **Wigmakers** *make their way across to* **Garrick**. *When the others in the room breathe out, the* **Wigmakers** *giggle as they are squeezed.*

Hunt   Mr Garrick, we would like an answer.

Mrs Garrick   What's it going to be like in the untamed wilds of Stratford? . . . It's near Scotland, isn't it?

Grimes   Near enough . . . I remember playing Glasgow.

Macklin   Ah, Glasgow's so close to hell.

Wheeler   Stratford's nowhere near Scotland.

Hunt   Mr Wheeler has an acute sense of geography.

Garrick *tries to eat his sandwiches whilst the* **Wigmakers** *try to put the wig on him and* **Grimes** *continues getting him into his costume.*

Garrick   Where's my hump? . . . it's dropped down! . . . it's like a carbuncle on my arse!

Grimes   Turn round!

Garrick   I can't.

Grimes   Everyone breathe in again.

All dutifully breathe in.

Mrs Garrick   The hump . . . push it up!

Grimes *and the* **Wigmakers** *push up* **Garrick**'s *hump.*

Macklin   I ask myself again, how could such a gifted thespian grow so unfashionable he has to knock his brains out in the cabbage-covered hinterland of England? I'd smite my breast in anguish but I don't want to muss up my only clean shirt. Remember the old days, Davey? . . . the freedom, the bonhomie, the money . . . my motto was 'don't have it if you can't have it good!' . . . expensive food, fine wines, grand houses . . . now all I have is dandruff. If it wasn't for the weight of responsibility to the drama, I'd give it all up.

Hunt   You've got to make a decision, Mr Garrick.

George Garrick   You can't ask my brother to make a decision just like that.

Grimes   He's an actor!

Macklin   As an actor he'll want to ponder, dither and doubt, consider, and cogitate before he says 'maybe', or even, 'perhaps'.

Rev. Jago   That could take for ever, if not longer. Why don't you make a choice, sir?

Garrick   Because I make thousands on stage every night. Do I move this way or that way? Do I roar that line like thunder or whisper it soft? Do I laugh there or weep here? Do I scowl or smile and lift my eyebrows? Down, up, left, right, sit, stand, go, stay, run, walk. Every choice means another set of choices and another and another, right down to how many curtain calls do I take? I leave the stage drained of choices.

A **Wardrobe Mistress** *forces her way in, holding up a jacket.*

Wardrobe Mistress   For you, Mr Garrick.

Mrs Garrick   Breathe in!

All breathe in as the **Wardrobe Mistress** *clambers past the others to get to* **Garrick**. *As they breathe out she gets stuck between* **Wheeler** *and* **Hunt**, *and has to pass the jacket over their heads.*

Hunt   Mr Garrick, could you please give us at least the hint of a decision before we leave?

Garrick   I'm a listener, first, last and always. Friends, should I take on this onerous task? Hands up all who say I shouldn't do it? . . . (*No one raises their hands.*) Hands up all those who say I should do it . . . (*Again no one raises their hands.*) No interest?

Mrs Garrick   No hands . . . we can't raise hands or anything else.

Wheeler *pushes himself up against the young* **Wigmaker**.

Wheeler   Speak for yourself!

Hunt   He's a lecherous wretch, unlike me.

Macklin   We're jammed, sir!

Mrs Garrick   It's up to you, David.

Garrick   If I have to make a judgement . . . alone . . . me, myself and I . . . then I come down decisively on 'perhaps' . . . on the one hand . . . on the other . . . it seems to me . . . if not now, when? . . . Judged in the balance and found . . . breathe in!

They all breathe in.

Garrick   The answer is 'no', I can't!

Macklin   You're in luck, gentlemen. I have an innate feeling for pageantry and I'm always dramatic. I even stab my potatoes at dinner. Charles Macklin – available for weddings, funerals, christenings and festivals, complete with speeches to tug the heartstrings, tickle the funnybone, and if the caterer needs an extra man, I can carry the chairs.

Rev. Jago   We didn't come for you, sir.

Macklin   But I've the voice for such occasions. It's trained to cut through the chatter of bored audiences, an incredibly flexible instrument that can shift from grovelling adulation to scabrous abuse in an instant; a mixture of unctuous vowels and specious authority.

Stage Manager's Voice   'Curtain up!'

They all let out their breath with a collective groan and stagger. The walls fall backwards to reveal they are only stage flats.

Garrick *rushes away upstage into the darkness. To the sound of applause the unseen* **Garrick** *begins his performance of* Richard III *whilst* **Mrs Garrick** *and the others untangle themselves.*

Hunt   This is terrible news.

George Garrick   Why terrible?

Rev. Jago   He can't come.

Macklin   It happens to us all . . . it happened to me.
Suddenly there was no call for the swirling cape, the low
bow and winning smile. It was over. Give my regards to
London, remember me to St James's Square.

George Garrick   He says 'no' now, but he'll change his
mind a hundred times before he says a final 'yes', 'no' or
'maybe'.

Garrick's Voice   'Now is the winter of our discontent /
Made glorious summer by this sun of York . . .'

Lights snap out.

Scene Three

Garrick *in a spot stage centre as Richard III, in a vague
approximation of Shakespeare's play.*

Garrick   And now – instead of riding fiery horses
And monsters from the deep
To frighten the souls of my enemies
I dance nimbly in a lady's chamber
To the wanton pleasing sound of a sinuous lute.

*As he dances, his hump has slipped down his tights, and now looks like
a huge carbuncle on his behind. As the audience laughs, he whirls
round, whips out a dagger and scuttles downstage and stuns them into
silence with his ferocity.*

But I that am curtail'd of this fair proportion
Cheated of feature by dissembling nature,
Deformed, unfinished, sent before my time
Into this breathing world, scarce half made up,
And that so lamely and unfashionable
That dogs bark at me, as I halt by them, –
Have no delight to pass away the time
Unless to see my shadow in the sun.

Spot out.

Scene Four

Lights up on a steam room. The large, naked **Samuel Johnson**
*lies on a table, half-covered by a towel, whilst a half-naked young
woman,* **Nell**, *massages him with her bare feet. Her movements are
rhythmic and turn into a dance on his back.*

Johnson   'For who would leave, unbribed Hibernia's
land, / Or change the rocks of Scotland for the Strand?' I
would, I would! . . . I lied when I wrote that, Mistress Nell.
All I was thinking of was a rhyme for 'land'.

Nell   You're a Grub Street scribbler, are you then, Doctor
Johnson?

Johnson   Yes, if you mean I write for money.

Nell   Who pays?

Johnson   The rich and powerful, Mistress Nell, which is
why I write in praise of the status quo.

Nell   What's the status quo?

Johnson   Things as they are.

Nell   Not as they should be?

Johnson   Fatal.

Nell *jumps off him.*

Nell   Would you like an enema, copulation, stimulation
. . . or a rub-down with a velvet glove?

David Garrick *rushes in stage right.*

Johnson   Take your clothes off, Davey, you're improperly
dressed.

Garrick   I've no time for such formalities. Why didn't you
come to the theatre last night? I expected you, looked for

you, we've been friends since schooldays. My performance was . . . damme, I don't use words lightly . . . 'astonishing'!

Johnson No one would miss a Garrick performance without good reason. I was up all night, finishing a piece for *The Rambler*.

Garrick In that case, I'll give you a taste of what you missed, and be damned to you . . . the last scene . . . enormous.

Johnson Stop him! . . . He's going to *act*! . . .

Nell *faints and* **Johnson** *heaves himself off the massage table, realises he is naked and quickly drapes a towel around himself.*

Johnson Sir, you nearly saw Samuel Johnson stark naked. That's a bigger spectacle than the death of Macbeth . . . and look what you've done to Mistress Nell.

Garrick *and* **Johnson** *bend down to help* **Nell**, *who sits up.*

Nell You're the famous player, Mr David Garrick!

Garrick Yes and this is Doctor Samuel Johnson, he's famous too.

Nell But he's not a playhouse player, is he? Would you write something for me, Mr Garrick . . . Nelly Fiske.

Garrick I've no pen or ink.

Nell Stay where you are, sir!

Nell *runs off.*

Garrick Did you see her faint? . . . they were doing that last night like winter flies. Only half of them stood up to applaud at the curtain, the rest were slumped on the ground. Shakespeare's mighty words had laid them out stony cold.

Johnson Shakespeare's words?! . . . half the speeches were your words, not Shakespeare's.

Garrick   You don't understand, Sam. Shakespeare unadulterated would be too strong for the delicate sensibilities of the times.

Nell *rushes back with a crayon.*

Nell   I couldn't find pen or ink . . . use this charcoal stick.

Garrick   On what, mistress?

Nell   Knickers!

Garrick   Knickers?

Nell *whips out a pair of knickers and hands them to* **Garrick**.

Nell   Sign!

*Garrick starts to write his name on her knickers, but finding he needs firm backing makes **Johnson** turn round. He spreadeagles the knickers on **Johnson**'s bare back, writes his name on them with a flourish and hands them back.*

Nell   David Garrick! . . . I've got David Garrick on my knickers! I'll be the toast of the stews of London.

She rushes off, clutching the knickers.

Johnson   This is the degradation of our age, sir. Pimping practitioners of Punch's mimic art frolic and posture on the dusty stage to universal recognition and applause.

Garrick   I didn't come to discuss my popularity, Sam, but to tell you I've been asked to organise a one-day Shakespeare's Jubilee in Stratford upon Avon. I haven't agreed one way or the other but I've sent brother George into the Warwickshire wilderness to scout possibilities. If I decide to accept, I'd like you to be my partner.

Johnson   Why me, sir?

Garrick   From our first days in Lichfield I've honoured you and you've endured me.

Johnson   It was all before us then, Davey lad. We had worlds to conquer . . . the answer's 'no'.

Garrick   Why not? You love Shakespeare almost as much as I. Your preface to the Master's plays lit the flame for his rebirth.

Johnson   That was scholarship, this is huckstering. You're listening to the clamour of the shilling gallery.

Garrick   Nothing wrong with that. I want his genius to spread. The danger is he could fall back into the swamp of universal neglect, and hear the dreaded cry 'out of print'!

Johnson   Veneration and idolatry are the real dangers. We fix our eyes on his graces and turn away from his deformities, and endure in him what we should, in another, loathe and despise.

Garrick   You *wrote* that . . . it's literary!

Johnson   Of course it's literary, sir! We're discussing literature, aren't we? You wish to turn Mr Shakespeare into a national celebrity. But celebrity wounds any sensitive artist, living or dead, by exposing their private person to public gaze. It forces that artist to share the same position as those who expose their cocks and arses in the street or swear in public places. The artist who becomes a celebrity has no privacy, the walls surrounding his life are glass. Little by little his clothes become flash, his actions, past and present, fall under the magnifying glass of fame: his soul dissolves. Celebrity gives the impression of valuing and supporting artists, in truth it only devalues and enfeebles them.

Garrick   But you've courted celebrity all your life. When you first came to London you were never off your knees.

Johnson   I was starving, my toes poked through my shoes. I don't crave it now. Let the works speak, Shakespeare's and mine. Celebrate the work, not the man. He needs no Jubilees.

Garrick   Master Boswell is writing a life of Samuel Johnson even as we speak.

Johnson   I console myself with the thought that no one will ever read it. David, reconsider. Some great writers should be left dozing on their shelves; they're too dangerous. Potent spirits lie imprisoned in their hard covers. They exert such a powerful spell, readers're bedazzled and bejinned. They're the last people to make sound judgements on their most loved author. They just want to place him on a high pedestal and gaze up at his blank, whitewashed face.

Garrick   You said, a man or woman who hasn't read Shakespeare is like someone who hasn't seen the ocean.

Johnson   I didn't say that, sir, but it's good enough to sound like me.

Garrick   Sam, Sam, join the Jubilee!

Johnson   Don't talk to me in those overtones, sir! I said no . . . no, no, no, no, no . . . N . . .O . . . no, no . . . it's a positive negative, i.e., no. Have I gone mute or are you going deaf? Jubilees! Jubilees! Why am I criss-crossed, it's enough to make a cat bark! . . . I'm counting the buttons, put white screens round the bed! . . . space furls, unfurls, spreads, shrinks . . . towels take wing . . . I stumble over Asia after all these years! . . . No Jubilee! . . . No Jubilee!

He falls into epileptic convulsions as lights snap out.

Scene Five

Stratford Greensward. Two sheep farmers, **Amos** *and* **Ted Ackers***, sit, surrounded by stuffed sheep.*

Amos Ackers   They can't take this land from us. It's common land, common Stratford folk've been grazing common sheep on it for generations. It's ours.

Ted Ackers   Nothing's ours 'less we fight for it. They want to make it the centre of a Jubilee they might be holding next Michaelmas Tuesday or whenever.

Amos Ackers   Haven't they stolen enough from us for one season, building the new Town Hall? . . . what's this Jubilee trick then, Ted?

Ted Ackers   It's in memory of a foreigner who lived in these parts once, called Bruce . . . no, I tell a lie . . . called Fred Shakespeare.

Amos Ackers   Never heard of Fred Shakespeare. There used to be a John and Mary Shakespeare lived out near Sprockets Farm. They had a boy called William, but he went bad.

Ted Ackers   Different person. This is Fred Shakespeare.

Amos Ackers   They can't ride roughshod or smoothshod over our ancient rights just because of a Fred Shakespeare.

Ted Ackers   They can and will. They've got the power. We don't count.

Amos Ackers   And can't read either.

George Garrick *enters.*

George Garrick   I'm George Garrick from London.

Ted Ackers   Ted and Amos Ackers, young sir.

George Garrick   Have you lived all your life in Stratford?

Ted Ackers   Twice that long.

Amos Ackers   Will you use this land for your Jubilee, Master Garrick?

George Garrick   Possibly. It's the only green patch in the centre of what passes as a town.

Ted Ackers   It belongs to the poor people of Stratford. We need it for our sheep.

George Garrick   Why aren't they moving?

Amos Ackers   They're stuffed.

Ted Ackers   Full of good grass. This is prime grazing land. They don't move 'cause they're contented, and fat!

Amos *pats a stuffed sheep.*

Amos Ackers   You're contented, aren't you, lad?

Ted Ackers   That's why we're not moving off this land for no Jubilee.

Amos Ackers   If you push us off the sheep'll starve and we'll starve.

George Garrick   Nobody wants you to do that.

Ted Ackers   But that's why you're here, isn't it?

George Garrick   I'm here because my brother, David, is thinking of running the Jubilee. I don't believe he should have anything to do with it.

Amos Ackers   So why've you come?

George Garrick   My brother asked me to scout out the possibilities.

Ted Ackers   I ask my brother to do things.

Amos Ackers   It rolls off my back like a duck.

Ted Ackers   And he don't ever want to. Of course it's vice versa, mickey-murky as well. I don't do anything he asks me to do.

George Garrick   It's different between David and me. It's a question of what he's got and I haven't – talent!

Amos Ackers   What's that?

George Garrick   A special gift and that gift needs to be nurtured so it flowers in glory. I attend to the nuts and bolts of his life so he can take his bows. Money, contracts, houses, servants, travel, his stinkin' undergarments, even his breath I sweeten nightly before he kisses his leading lady. I know my price, I could do better elsewhere, but ties of blood hold me fast . . . (*The sheep 'baa' loudly in agreement.*) They agree.

David owes it all to me. He had the talent but, as you said, what's that? It has to be brought forth to shine. I make it happen. Even now, there are hundreds of Davids called Jack, living in Somerset unsung. But thanks to me, the public listen to him though he won't listen to me. I'll make him. This, the armpit of England, called Stratford's no place to hold a Jubilee now or ever. Your common land is safe. I swear it.

Amos Ackers   Hear that, my woolly sweets!

Ted Ackers   Grow fat. The wolves won't be coming down from the hills this winter.

The sheep, which are on wheels, are pulled off 'baa-baaing' loudly.

Lights out.

Scene Six

*Lights up on **Garrick**'s bedroom. **Garrick** and **Mrs Garrick** are getting ready for bed.*

Mrs Garrick   What did Samuel say about the Stratford project?

Garrick   He had a fit when I mentioned it.

Mrs Garrick   George has reported Stratford isn't good enough to hold a cockfight. We're all against it, Samuel, George, me and Grimes.

Garrick   I don't care what Grimes thinks.

Mrs Garrick   Don't forget he played Glasgow, and won.

Garrick   I only regret the journeys I never started. It's another chance for glory, my dear.

Mrs Garrick   Yesterday Charles Macklin was where you are today. Now he has frayed cuffs and dandruff on his collar. He's forced to eat the bread of desolation and tour the provinces. Worse, his heart's frosted over. Think on him, Davey. He rose so high, his feet finally didn't touch the ground, and then he fell.

They get into bed.

Garrick   I remember seeing you for the first time . . . you were in a white dress with a bunch of forget-me-nots pinned to your heart . . . I was outside in the rain and you had a dark ribbon in your hair and drinking hot chocolate . . . you looked up at me.

Mrs Garrick   You'll lose money if you do it.

Garrick   No, the townsfolk are financing the whole venture.

Mrs Garrick   They're tradesmen, they have very small pockets and hate dipping into them.

Garrick   Gad, you could be right. It could cost me!

Mrs Garrick   Not 'could' – will!

Garrick   I won't do it!

Mrs Garrick   You're still worried, Davey. Try not to dream.

Garrick   Oh, but in dreams I write epics, have no trouble swimming underwater, see two suns and four moons and talk to birds, particularly swans and penguins.

Mrs Garrick   Go to sleep . . . lie soft, my love and sleep secure.

He kisses her and blows out the light. Voices are heard in the darkness. Someone curses as they stumble.

Hands' Voice   I can't see anything, Trevor.

Nunn's Voice   You should feel comfortable, Terry. It's as dimly lit as one of your productions.

Hall's Voice   Audience can never see a damn thing, even if they wanted to.

Hands' Voice   Directors always walk into rooms voice first, Peter.

Hall's Voice   But no one can see our faces!

Nunn's Voice   Good God!

Garrick *lights a candle to reveal the figures of* **Peter Hall**, **Terry Hands** *and* **Trevor Nunn**, *in modern clothes, standing by the bed.*

Garrick   Who're you?

Nunn   Dream figures. You're dreaming us now. I'm Trevor Nunn, Commander of the British Empire . . . this is Sir Peter Hall, and this is Sir . . . this is Mr Terry . . .

Hands   Hands . . . plain Hands and proud of it. I haven't compromised for empty titles, age-old baubles, Sir This, Lord That. You two carry the mark of Cain.

Garrick   What do you want?

Hall   We're future directors of the Royal Shakespeare Company Theatre, Stratford. We've entered your dreams to thank you. From this Jubilee there'll spring a worldwide Shakespeare industry. It's a million-dollar enterprise.

Nunn   You started it all.

Garrick   No, I didn't. I want nothing to do with the project.

Hands   I'm appalled! It's so selfish. What about us? We need the money.

Nunn   And the prestige. Of course, I won't starve, cold winter nights, thanks to my 'memories'.

Hall   If you don't say 'yes', there'll be no Shakespeare Jubilee, no Memorial Theatre, no plays, no money and no prestige.

Nunn   Those plays're our bread and butter. We'd be lost. The state spends millions promoting Shakespeare every year. He's on the school curriculum so he has a guaranteed audience, which he wouldn't have if he wasn't part of our national heritage. Without Shakespeare they'd have to rethink the whole educational system.

Hands   He's basic. Without him we'd have to put on new plays, rediscovered old ones. We might even have to get different jobs. But we've no training, no experience, no aptitude.

Nunn   I don't know about that, Terry. I mean, I could become a film director.

Hands   Oh, yes . . . dream on, Trevor.

Hall   I've tried and it isn't easy, believe me . . . do you realise, Mr Garrick, without Shakespeare I wouldn't be able to live in the style to which I'm accustomed.

Garrick   I'm sorry.

Hands   Sorry doesn't cut it. Everything depends on you. You lit the flame that blazoned the name William Shakespeare across the world stage and into every village, every town, every city, every hamlet.

Hall   He wrote a great play called *Hamlet.* I once interviewed dozens of actors for the part, but none of them had the legs for it.

Garrick   The Jubilee's too risky. I can't lose money.

Hall   That's something I can understand.

Nunn   We can all understand. It's a terrible thing.

Hall   I've always believed the easiest way to save money on a production is not to use your own.

Hands   We all know the value of money, particularly Mr CBE. He's a man of rare gifts, only nobody's ever got one from him. Trevor's the only person I know who wouldn't give a tip to a rabbi at a circumcision.

Nunn   That's rubbish, Terry, and you know it! When an actor's been working with the Company for ten years I always throw a testimonial coffee break, at my own expense.

Hall   We're all very good with actors, I have to say. I always tell my lot . . . 'this is only a suggestion, but don't let's forget who's making it'.

Nunn   I like my actors to come right out and say exactly what they think, when they agree with me.

Hands   You have to admire him, Mr Garrick, if you don't you're fired.

Hall   To get back to the matter in hand, you won't lose money, Mr Garrick, and you'll come out of it smelling of roses.

Garrick   How do you know?

Nunn   We're from the future. You'll be bigger and richer than ever if you take our advice.

Hands   We're giving you the straight stuff, Mr G. If you sponsor the Jubilee, your fame will live forever, with the Bard's.

Hall   ⎫   (*singing softly*)   'Shakespeare, Shakespeare,
Nunn   ⎬   Shakespeare you can hear us cry / As the
Hands   ⎭   Bard of Avon, sweeps us upwards to the sky /
We'll be sitting pretty, we can do no wrong / All you have to do is string along.'

The voices can be heard harmonising in the darkness.

Scene Seven

Lights up on **Garrick** *alone on the Drury Lane Stage. He comes downstage centre.*

Garrick   Hit me! . . . (*A spotlight hits him.*) Why am I me? Why not a mortician? Why not a goldfish in a goldfish bowl? I'm like the Tinker of Exeter who comforted himself on the gallows with the words: 'I've done something to have my name talked of in this world.' He was content as he dingled-dangled; he was paying the agreed price for his moment of fame. Stratford will increase mine, so haul me higher!

George Garrick, **Grimes**, *and* **Mrs Garrick** *usher in* **Wheeler**, **Hunt** *and the* **Rev. Jago**.

Hunt   We were on our way home, sir.

Rev. Jago   A playhouse stage is no place for an ordained Minister of the Church.

Grimes   This is the Drury Lane stage, Reverend. Hallowed ground, children half-price.

Mrs Garrick   Can't you see ghosts hanging in the haunted air? All waiting for an actor to give them life again, so they can rant and rave and suffer for our delight.

Rev. Jago   Not my delight, madam. I hate the theatre and all who sail in her. I can say it now we've lost your husband!

He, **Hunt** *and* **Wheeler** *attempt to exit but find they are frozen in position.*

Hunt   We can't move!

Garrick   Of course, I haven't given you your exit lines yet.

Grimes   Sorry, gents, he's the star.

Garrick   I had a dream last night.

Mrs Garrick I shouldn't've baked you that cheese and onion pie for supper.

Garrick I was visited by three witches or three kings, frankly I'm not sure what they were.

Grimes Did they come bearing gifts?

Garrick No, they were empty-handed. They looked like men who would never stand their round. Perhaps it was because they were facing destitution. Not a pretty sight. I know, I've been there, too. Worse than destitution, they were facing obscurity if I didn't sponsor the First Shakespeare Jubilee. They begged me even though they knew the Jubilee was to take place in stinky Stratford.

Hunt 'Stinky'?! If I were a younger man, in better shape and taller, I'd challenge you to a duel!

Rev. Jago 'Stinky' is too much to bear. Give us our exit lines, sir!

Garrick If I did you wouldn't hear me say a one-day Jubilee Festival for seventeen sixty-nine is out . . . but I will lead and organise a three-day Jubilee Festival!

Hunt, **Wheeler** and **Rev. Jago** *'unfreeze'*.

Hunt In that case, Stratford *is* stinky.

Rev. Jago Indubitably.

George Garrick You can't do it!

Mrs Garrick and **George Garrick** *pull* **Garrick** *to one side*.

George Garrick It means more work, more trouble. We survived the theatre riots of sixty-two, now you want more of the same.

Mrs Garrick Why three days for the Jubilee instead of just one?

George Garrick   Hubris, David, hubris, and you know what follows hubris – nemesis.

Garrick   Aristotle never had to open on a wet night in Wigan. It's three days because three prophets came to me, dreaming, not one. Besides, three gives us more chance to make an impact. I know it's a big risk and I understand why you both wouldn't want to follow me on this one.

Mrs Garrick   I will because I love you. What's your excuse, George?

George Garrick   I can never see what's on the other side of the wall or imagine what a flame looks like after it's been blown out. So your visions fill my days, David. But I fight it.

Garrick *puts his arms round* **Mrs Garrick** *and* **George Garrick**.

Garrick   We happy few, we band of brothers. That fought with us upon St Crispin's day . . . George, mobilise the foot soldiers, designers, composers, musicians, wigmakers; Eva, inform the *Public Advertiser* and the *London Evening Post*. Grimes, spread the word amongst the seedier sort. I'll tell His Majesty of our great plans!

He exits with **George Garrick** *and* **Mrs Garrick**.

Wheeler   His Majesty? He's going to tell the King?

Hunt   Will he invite him to the Jubilee, do you think? I didn't realise it might become a royal event.

Rev. Jago   We've never met royalty. How do we act? We're simple country folk from the nether regions.

Grimes   You can learn. Sure, I'm descended meself from Queen Maeve and the kings of old Ireland. Me mother had a royal cloak, finely woven as a plover's wing it was, that once hung from the shoulders of Irish royalty and now finding in our house a second glory.

Hunt   We might learn but what about our wives? Mine is as refined as a cabbage.

Wheeler The sound of mine drinking beer in a tavern last week made five couples get up and dance.

Rev. Jago The only uplifting thing about mine is her bust. They haven't the social graces. But neither have we. Look at my feet!

Grimes I'll teach you how to treat royalty, for a suitable fee. I meet royalty on a regular basis so I know. Remember the English have etiquette not manners. If you don't know how to eat your buttered parsnips, you're out!

Garrick *re-enters, in a coat.*

Garrick Where's my carriage? What're you doing, Grimes?

Grimes Trying to supplement the meagre wages you don't pay me. They've never met a king. I'm teaching them how.

Garrick I've met dozens in my time, here, on this stage . . . two Richards, two Henrys and a John. Watch listen, learn . . .

Garrick *impersonates in rapid succession, five Shakespearean kings. First he capers about, dragging his leg as Richard III.*

Garrick 'Now is the winter of our discontent / Made glorious summer by this sun of York . . .' (*He falls on the ground as Richard II.*) 'Let's talk of graves, of worms and epitaphs; / Make dust our paper, and with rainy eyes / Write sorrow on the bosom of the earth . . .' (*He jumps up, heroically, as Henry V.*) 'Once more into the breach, dear friends, once more; / Or close the wall up with our English dead! . . .' (*He looks round furtively as King John.*) 'It is the curse of kings to be attended / By slaves that take their humours for a warrant / To break within the bloody house of life . . .' (*As Henry VIII he puts his hands on his hips, and stands with his legs apart, and roars.*) 'No, sir, it does not please me. / I had thought I had had men of some understanding / And wisdom of my council; but I find none . . .' There, gentlemen, I've given you five kings, two more than the infant Jesus met.

Grimes   Totally useless for what they want. They won't be meeting any Richard II or III, Henry V or VIII, or even a King John. They'll be facing the breeches-pissing George III, an entirely different bag of nuts. I'll play George III. You three approach, bow and address me as 'Your Majesty'.

Hunt, **Wheeler** *and* **Rev. Jago** *start to bow.*

Garrick   No, no. When encountering royalty, the bow must be as elegant and deep as possible. First, slide the leading foot forward, bending the back at the same time, and rise on the 'scraping foot'. Then a short step sideways on to the right foot, removing your hat gracefully. Now, bow the back, not at right angles, but to appear rounded. After that, you're on your own.

Hunt, **Wheeler** *and* **Rev. Jago** *get themselves into a terrible tangle as they attempt to follow* **Garrick's** *instructions.*

Grimes   It needs work. Just do your clod-hopping Stratford bows for now.

He assumes a royal pose. **Hunt**, **Wheeler** *and* **Rev. Jago** *bow clumsily.*

Hunt
Wheeler   } Your Majesty.
Rev. Jago

Grimes *as GEORGE III burps loudly and dribbles.*

Grimes   Knaves, fools, you're niffy-naffy fellows from the 'Frog and Toad', hostelry for drunken sots . . . quick, grab it, there's a knighthood galloping past!

He starts crying loudly. **Hunt**, **Wheeler** *and* **Rev. Jago** *look embarrassed.*

Wheeler   What do we say now?

Garrick   This is His Majesty, George III of England.
Make small talk whilst he farts and pisses, shits and
shambles his way to oblivion. Be chic in his presence. He's
the peak, the pinnacle of our society; king of the hill! Try it
again.

Hunt
Wheeler } Your Majesty.
Rev. Jago

Grimes *breaks wind.*

Grimes   Did someone step on a duck?

Hunt   Wittily put, sire.

Wheeler   Delightful, sire.

Grimes   Before you came in I just died. But my doctors
described my condition as satisfactory . . . if you won't leave
me alone I'll find someone who can . . . (*He runs around like a
chicken.*) . . . God has his eye on me . . . He's in my trousers!
Open the back door and let Him out!

Garrick   Avaunt! Avaunt!

He and **Grimes** *exit, dancing.* **Hunt**, **Wheeler** *and* **Rev.
Jago** *exit dancing in a line behind him.*

Scene Eight

Garrick'*s temple to Shakespeare in the grounds of his Hampton
house. There is a bust of Shakespeare, which looks a lot like* **Garrick**
*himself, in a niche and Shakespearean memorabilia in glass cases:
white gloves, shoehorn, inkstand and manuscript. A chair made of
mulberry wood stands in the centre as* **George Garrick** *spins
round and round.*

George Garrick   Careful you don't fall . . . spot and
focus . . . I'm being sucked down into his whirlpool . . . I
must break free . . . (*He stops spinning.*) Even when we were
children I was different from him. I preferred to leave early,

to knock on wood, dogs to cats, trees to rivers and green to
blue. Mother said we could've been strangers, we were so
different.

Garrick *hurries in.*

Garrick   The Poet Laureate's just written a poem
dedicated to me . . . 'A nation's taste depends on you /
Perhaps a nation's virtue too.'

George Garrick   Cock-a-doodle do! Cock-a-doodle do!
(*He flaps his arms up and down like a rooster.*)

Garrick   What're you saying, brother?

George Garrick   You're sacrificing all our hard-won
respect by this Jubilee folly.

Garrick *walks round the temple touching the memorabilia.*

Garrick   Here in this temple devoted to the Bard I have
the First Quarto of *Hamlet*. A scribe transcribed his very own
words. Each letter from his own pen to this pen. From his
eyes to my eyes . . . (*He strokes the chair.*) A chair carved from
the mulberry tree he planted . . . (*Singing*) 'All shall yield to
the mulberry tree. / Bend to thee / Blest mulberry tree. /
Matchless was he / Who planted thee, / And thou, like him,
immortal be' . . . this shoehorn, this inkstand, these gloves,
Shakespeare's own, given to John Ward by a descendant of
the Bard.

He puts on the gloves and sits in the chair.

George Garrick   Davey, confess it, you want to link
Shakespeare's immortality with your own.

Garrick   Like most, I don't want to die. Actors're fêted in
their brief day but poets endure till the earth turns cold. My
words die in the air, those written will last till the manuscript
crumbles. I want to be part of that.

George Garrick   But a tawdry Jubilee, with pageants,
glees, sideshows, cheap-jacks and fireworks isn't worthy of
us.

Garrick   George, my official debut was as Richard III
when the town went horn-mad for me. But my first
appearance on stage was as Harlequin. I love glees,
fireworks, cheap-jacks and the rest of the floating world. I'm
both Richard and Harlequin . . . this memorabilia,
Shakespeare's manuscript, shoehorn, inkstand, chair,
gloves're most likely fakes. This chair I'm sure is one. There
isn't enough authentic mulberry wood left to carve a
midget's toothpick. This is simulated mulberry wood.
Infinitely more expensive than the real thing, but still fake.
And I sat for that bust. It's more me than Shakespeare. But
I believe, because I want to believe, knowing they're fake I
believe they're real, touched by the master. The same with
the Jubilee. It may be a vulgar jamboree but 'twill still
honour the love of my life. We'll make it the most
remarkable event in the history of the theatre.

George Garrick   We will? You will, Davey.

Garrick   No, 'we'. I need you, brother. I've always
needed you. The triumph will be but ashes if you're not by
my side.

He rises and puts his arm round **George**'s *shoulders.* **George
Garrick** *looks at his brother.*

George Garrick   You're such a devilish good actor, even
I don't know when you're acting and when you're not.

Garrick   You don't? *I* don't! There's no difference acting
and not acting, it's all one to me. Even when I'm not acting,
I'm acting not acting; so where are you? Spread the good
word, brother. George and Davey Garrick're on the march!

Lights out to their singing together.

Garrick   } 'All shall yield to the mulberry tree. /
George Garrick   Bend to thee / Blest mulberry tree. /
Matchless was he / Who planted thee, / And those, like
him, immortal be.'

Scene Nine

Mrs Ross's salon. Drapes unroll from the flies. A sofa and table, with tea-cups, are pushed on by a **Maid***. There are two doors, one upstage centre, and one stage left.* **Mrs Ross***, a small, middle-aged woman, comes in with* **George Garrick** *and* **Lydia***.* **George** *and* **Mrs Ross** *sit on the sofa whilst* **Lydia** *takes tea at the table.*

George Garrick   My brother, David, will be hosting a Shakespeare Jubilee Festival this September. We'll be putting a notice in the best broadsheets but in the end, word of mouth is more important for an event like this.

Mrs Ross   You think I can do more good than the *Chronicle*?

George Garrick   Come, come, Mrs Ross, your salon is the finest in London. Your clientele is the crème de la crème.

Mrs Ross   Even if they look as though they've been stuffed by a good taxidermist, I do have the upper part of the upper crust.

George Garrick   That's why you were my first port of call, to spread the good word. You have the sort of people we want to come to Stratford.

Lydia   They all try to come here.

Mrs Ross   Lydia, the reason you get a stabbing pain in your right eye when you drink tea is because you haven't taken the spoon out of the cup. I'm trying to teach you ladies' etiquette.

Lydia   We appreciate it, Mrs Ross, but what good's etiquette at an orgy? You just don't know who to thank.

Mrs Ross   You can always be relied on to hit the nail squarely on the thumb . . . try some fan-talk, Lydia . . .

Lydia *brings out a fan and follows instructions.*

Mrs Ross   Say 'Hush we are overheard' . . . (**Lydia** *puts the closed fan tip to her lips.*) That's good . . . now say 'yes' . . . (**Lydia** *puts the fan to her right cheek.*) Now, 'no'.

Lydia   I never say 'no'.

Mrs Ross   Say 'You're welcome' . . . (**Lydia** *extends her right hand, palm up.*) 'I love you' . . . (*The open fan hides her eyes.*) 'Get lost' . . . (**Lydia** *makes a sweeping movement with the open fan.*) Which is something I'm inclined to say to you, George, with or without a fan. Why should I help your brother? This Jubilee will decimate London society. All the best people will want to be seen in Stratford, not in my salon. Lydia, time to get dressed for work.

Lydia *carefully puts down her fan and calmly undresses to her underwear.* **Mrs Ross** *and* **George** *pay no attention.*

George Garrick   I can see you might be worried about loss of trade, Mrs Ross, so why don't you come to Stratford? The country gentry could do with a touch of metropolitan sophistication only you can provide.

Mrs Ross   Bringing this degree of sophistication to the outer reaches of Warwickshire might be too much for them. Could they stand the shock? More important, could their pockets?

George Garrick   Rich pickings there, Mrs Ross, rich pickings.

Hermione *enters to collect* **Lydia**'s *dress. She is about to leave with it when she notices the others are staring at her.*

Hermione   Well?

Mrs Ross   You never leave a room without saying something. Nowadays maids, servants, flunkeys, first and second attendants, all want to be heard.

George Garrick   I see it on stage every night. The English like maids and butlers to know their comic place.

But now, it seems, every spear-carrying menial must have their moment in the sun.

Hermione   Since you asked, why celebrate Shakespeare? What if some poets soar high enough to hear the music of the spheres and write it down and Shakespeare is one such transcriber? While you celebrate him, the real world is being forgotten for a verb or a noun. Life . . . listen to me . . . life is a series of lessons which must be lived through to be understood. What does Shakespeare know of the terror of my life, a slave to fetching and carrying? Don't cry over his verse, cry over my life. Celebrate me, not that scribbler who lies rotting in the earth. He doesn't need your flags and trumpets. Celebrate me! Celebrate me!

She exits.

Mrs Ross   I don't know what I'd do without her, but I'd rather.

Lydia   One thing I don't understand. What is Shakespeare for?

Mrs Ross   He fills us with compassion for all God's creatures. After seeing a Shakespeare play, we are wiser, kinder, happier, bushier.

Lydia   Bushier?

Mrs Ross   Bushier. I owe my magnificent head of hair to the days I've spent watching Shakespeare.

Lord Dorset, *his gouty right foot swathed in bandages, hobbles in upstage centre, leaning on* **Charmaine**, *another beautiful, undressed woman.*

Lord Dorset   (*singing*) 'Here's to the soldier and his arms / Fall in, fall in./Here's to the woman and her arms / Fall in, fall in! . . .' I'm glad you're free tonight, Charmaine.

Charmaine   Why do you always ask for me, my lord?

Lord Dorset   Because you've got something I like.

Charmaine   What's that?

Lord Dorset   Patience . . . you find me a touch downcast, Mrs Ross. I gave the performance of my life in bed last night. I'm just sorry my wife wasn't awake. George, I hear your brother is staging some Jubilee in the first week of September. Can't do it, sir, can't! It's bang in the middle of Shrewsbury Race Week.

George Garrick   That's why we picked it, Lord Dorset. Racegoers can sample our Jubilee delights.

Lydia   And ours. We'll be there, won't we, Mrs Ross?

Lord Dorset   Put me down for a ticket then, Master George!

They hear a loud, braying laugh.

George Garrick   It's him!

Lord Dorset   Run for your lives!

Mrs Ross   Too late!

James Boswell *enters upstage centre, drunk.*

Boswell   I'm James Boswell, and you're not! Ah, Lord Dorset, your gout still troubling you?

Lord Dorset   Ahhhhh!

Boswell *has accidentally stepped on* **Lord Dorset**'s *bandaged foot.*

Lydia   Why aren't you in Scotland?

Boswell   I'm here for that bosom, that tongue, that lip, that hair, that petticoat, that ribbon, that glove, that slipper, that heel, that giggle, that smile, that dream, that shadow, that enchantment. I don't remember your face but your breath is familiar.

Mrs Ross   Now I know why tigers eat their young. To what do we owe the pleasure?

Lord Dorset   What pleasure?

Charmaine   I'll show you. (*She takes him upstage. They go through the door stage left.*)

Boswell   I'm down from the granite hills of Scotland to hear news, gossip, scandal and savour the fashions of the town and see a hanging or two. I do so like a good hanging. I hear there's to be a Jubilee in a place called Stratford.

George Garrick   No, you've been misinformed.

Boswell   I'm disappointed. When I hear the word culture, I reach for my purse. We don't get much of it in Scotland, though the blessings of civilisation creep on apace. They have cold water toilets, lamp lights and parcel post twice daily in Edinburgh.

Boswell *suddenly lurches over and flings open the door upstage left to show a tableau of a startled* **Lord Dorset**, *shielding his naked foot and* **Charmaine** *entangled in bandages.*

Boswell   Scotland's the coming place! Parcel post!

He slams the door shut and brays with laughter, falls on his knees and pitches forward, unconscious.

George Garrick   If Samuel Johnson has to rely on this Scottish sot for posthumous fame, he'll be forgotten a week after his death. What do we do with him?

Mrs Ross   I usually put him in a cupboard to sleep it off.

George Garrick   But he'll still be in London when he wakes. He'll find out about the Jubilee and once the best people hear James Boswell's coming, they won't!

Mrs Ross   Send him back to Scotland.

George Garrick   He won't go.

Mrs Ross *crosses upstage centre and shouts.*

Mrs Ross   Hermione, sheets of wrapping paper, string and sealing wax! . . . (*She knocks on the door upstage left.*) Cease the hydraulics, I need your help! George, get him on to the table.

Boswell *has become rigid as* **Mrs Ross**, **Lydia** *and* **George** *lift him on to the table and lay him on his back. A dishevelled* **Lord Dorset** *and* **Charmaine** *emerge as* **Hermione** *enters upstage centre with brown wrapping paper, string, sealing wax and bottles of wine.*

Mrs Ross   Give me a hand, so I can slide some sheets of wrapping paper under him.

They lift **Boswell** *so* **Mrs Ross** *can lay the large sheets of paper under him.*

Lord Dorset   What're we doing, Madam?

Mrs Ross   Sending James Boswell home to Scotland.

George Garrick   How?

Mrs Ross   By parcel post.

Lydia   Parcel post?

Mrs Ross   You heard, there's now a regular, reliable postal service from London to Edinburgh. So we're posting him.

Lord Dorset *and* **George** *take a deep drink, then pass the bottles to* **Lydia**, **Charmaine** *and* **Hermione**. **Mrs Ross** *tries to wrap the brown paper over* **Boswell**, *but his raised knees make it difficult.*

Lord Dorset   What if he wakes up before he gets there?

Mrs Ross   He'll be out for twelve hours at least. And even if he wakes, he won't be in London.

George Garrick   Let me give you a hand!

Mrs Ross   We've got to straighten him first, so we can wrap him properly. Press his knees down.

But as **George** *and* **Lord Dorset** *press down on* **Boswell**'s *knees, his head and torso jerk up.*

Lord Dorset   Charmaine, sit on his face, whilst we press.

Charmaine   Why is it me sitting on his face?

Mrs Ross   No one else can do it with such finesse.

Charmaine   But he's unconscious. He won't appreciate it.

Lord Dorset   We will!

As the others agree, **Hermione** *puts a chair at the head of the table.* **Charmaine** *climbs on it and sits on* **Boswell***'s upturned face.*

Lydia   You're going to charge him for the service, aren't you, Mrs Ross?

Mrs Ross   Of course. It's a speciality of the house. Start pressing, gentlemen.

Lord Dorset *and* **George** *press down on* **Boswell***'s raised knees.* **Boswell***'s head jerks up and bounces* **Charmaine***, sitting on top of his face.*

Charmaine   Ooohh!

Mrs Ross   Press down harder, Charmaine.

As **Charmaine** *presses down, there is a loud snap as* **Boswell** *finally lies straight with his knees down.* **Charmaine** *gets off* **Boswell***'s face as* **Mrs Ross** *looks at him.*

Mrs Ross   I do believe he's smiling . . . Hermione, pen and ink.

As **Hermione** *exits quickly upstage, they completely wrap* **Boswell** *in brown paper, and tie him up like a parcel.* **Hermione** *comes back with ink and quill pen, a lighted candle and sealing stamp.* **Charmaine** *melts the sealing wax as the string knots round the wrapped* **Boswell***.* **Lydia** *takes the seal.*

Lydia   Let me, Mrs Ross, let me!

Lydia *gleefully stamps the soft wax.*

George Garrick   Is that your own personal seal, Mrs Ross?

Mrs Ross   Yes, a stag rampant.

Lord Dorset   We can't do this! It's madness. Whatever we think of the man, we can't post him into the unknown. We haven't got his address.

Mrs Ross   I have. Twenty-seven Caledonian Mews, Edinburgh, Scotland.

Lord Dorset   Oh, that's all right, then. Carry on!

Mrs Ross   Ladies, go and find a trolley.

Lydia, **Charmaine** and **Hermione** *exit upstage centre whilst* **George Garrick** *writes* **Boswell**'s *name and address on the parcel.*

Lord Dorset   Gad, your calligraphy's beautiful, George. Mine looks like chicken scratches.

Lydia, **Charmaine** and **Hermione** *come back with a trolley.* **George** *finishes addressing the parcel, and they lift it on to the trolley.*

Mrs Ross   The postal authorities can weigh and stamp him but he should be collected right away.

Lord Dorset   You're creating the right conditions for a successful Jubilee, George. Encouraging the best people and banning the rest.

Lydia, **Charmaine**, **George Garrick** and **Lord Dorset** *push the trolley and the parcel out upstage centre as the lights dim.*

Scene Ten

Spot up on **Mrs Ross** *and* **Hermione** *as they sit at the table, finishing the wine.*

Mrs Ross   Why do they try to light up Shakespeare's name? Fame scatters her poppies in the memory of man without regard to merit. Herostratus burnt down the temple of Diana and lives for ever. The name of the man who built it is lost. When William is festooned with garlands, other Williams sleep in everlasting night. It's a kind of madness to trumpet one such William, when so many've gone down without a whisper.

Hermione   They aren't doing it for William Shakespeare, but for themselves. If he lives, perhaps they will too. It's natural. It's the wish of every human being not to be forgotten. The universal secret, from which all other secrets spring, is the longing for more, much more life. But immortality lasts a generation for most of us. We're remembered, if at all, by our children. We're buried in our sons and daughters. Generations pass while trees grow tall. It's vanity to think any names should last.

Mrs Ross   Don't they see, if a poet's fame is built for longer lasting, it needs no artificial preservation. Their Jubilee monuments are Jubilee pyramids of snow. They can't fight the opium of time.

Hermione   And if they do, what of it? If William is spared by time he'll probably be consumed by avarice. He'll become a product to be sold on street corners with the cry 'Snake oil, snake oil, get your Shakespeare snake oil, the universal balm and cure-all!'

Mrs Ross   What if the whole world knew of Shakespeare? Say his fame extended to the Antipodes, what's that, when not a quarter of his own countrymen remember him? Say they all did, what's that to the world? And even if the whole world knew of him, what's that to the stars? For if the stars be infinite and every star has a sun and every sun has planets about it, what proportion would know the name of Shakespeare?

Hermione   How many poets wrote in former ages and yet the works of scarce – what? – one in ten thousand remain. Neither their books nor their bodies persist and after every Jubilee their shadows're no longer than before.

Mrs Ross Men're too weak to face the truth, women can. We begin to die the moment we begin. Our days add up by tiny accumulations to one long night.

Hermione And we'll never know what song the Sirens sang, or what name Achilles used when he hid himself amongst the women.

Spot out.

Scene Eleven

Mrs Garrick *is heard singing in the darkness.*

Mrs Garrick's Voice (*singing*) 'Let beauty with the sun arise / Let Shakespeare tribute pay / With heavenly smiles and sparkling eyes / Give grace and glory to the day.'

Lights up on **Garrick***'s living room.* **Mrs Garrick** *stands by the young composer,* **Charles Dibdin***, at the piano.*

Mrs Garrick It's beautiful, Charles.

Dibdin You make it beautiful, Eva Maria. It's called 'Dawn Serenade' because it's be to sung on the first day of the Jubilee by a chorus of golden nymphs. I've been a slave to it for weeks. I said to your husband, 'I don't know what to do with it' and he said, 'Do something and then we can fix it.' I struggle to find melodies that can be picked up at one hearing but your husband can't hold a tune, even if it has handles. He's paying me twenty guineas to set all his Jubilee lyrics but it'll cost me twenty-five for the trip to Stratford. That's the dirty sub-text of theatre. The ugly truth is that though music is the most ethereal and abstract of all the arts, it begins and ends in money . . . *do*, ray, me, fah, soh, la, te, *do* . . . it's dough at both ends.

Garrick *hurries in stage left, flourishing a sheaf of papers.*

Garrick   My 'Ode to Shakespeare'. The centrepiece of the whole Jubilee. You must hear it, my dear. You too, Charles.

Dibdin   First my 'Dawn Serenade'.

Mrs Garrick   It's beautiful, David.

Garrick   I'm sure it is, my dear. But first my Ode . . . 'To what blest genius of the isle. . .'

But **Dibdin** *has already started playing and singing the 'Dawn Serenade' as* **Grimes** *enters upstage centre with* **Dr Thomas Arne**.

Grimes   Doctor Thomas Arne, the foremost composer of his time.

Dibdin   Who says so?

Grimes   He does. Kept insisting I announce him as old Tom Arne, the foremost etc. etc.

Grimes *exits upstage centre.*

Dibdin   Who invited this man?

Garrick   I did. He's writing the music to my Ode. The one that begins 'To what blest genius . . .'

Dibdin   I was going to write that! I have more talent in my smallest fart than he has in his whole body.

Dr Arne   You had a narrow escape, Garrick, his last song was written to be played through tissue paper, stretched over a comb. His music stinks to the ear.

Dibdin   Oh, very good! I must jot that down.

Dr Arne   Do. There's just enough room on your forehead.

Dibdin   This man plays the violin like the strings were still in the cat!

Garrick   Charles, you do the popular songs, the glees, rounds, and choruses, whilst Dr Arne devotes himself to my Ode, 'To what blest genius . . .'

Dr Arne   I'm inspired already. The music will be uplifting, transcendental.

Dibdin   And dull. Listen to my 'Dawn Serenade' and hear how piss-poor words should be set.

Dr Arne   This from the man who wrote a song called 'I'd Like to be a Sister to a Brother Just Like You'.

Grimes *returns upstage centre.*

Grimes   May I introduce Mr George Steevens, scholar, wit, renowned critic and tight-arse.

George Steevens *enters.*

Mrs Garrick   Why did you let that man in, Grimes?

Grimes   He used violence. He forced two guineas into my pocket. I was helpless.

He exits upstage centre.

Steevens   Dear lady, why this fury?

Mrs Garrick   You attacked my husband in print.

Dr Arne   You know nothing about music.

Dibdin   Or singing.

Garrick   Or acting.

Steevens   Of course not. I'm a critic. I have no qualifications at all. When I go into a playhouse I know nothing about what's going on there, or why. I have no prejudices. I'm a total blank.

Garrick   You're a total blank when you go in and when you come out. You've learnt nothing, felt nothing, except the paltry fee the newspaper pays you as a critic.

Mrs Garrick   I know you, sir, you're here to sneer at the carpets.

Steevens   No, I'm on a peace mission. I've persuaded the *Westminster Gazette* to let me write a series of pieces on the Jubilee.

Dibdin   But you're against it.

Steevens   You know my views of this Shakespeare of yours. I believe he uses exalted language to make terrible situations bearable, beautiful, even touching. The pain melts away in a golden syrup of words. And what words. 'Violentest', 'lyingest', 'infortunate', 'incertain', 'incivil', 'unviolable', 'unfallible', 'unseeming', 'sudden-bold', 'more-elder', 'more-worst' . . . And the grammar! An adverb can be used as a verb, 'They askance their eyes' . . . or as an adjective verb. He can 'happy' your friends, 'malice' your enemies, or 'fall' an axe on your head. Anything goes and goes it does . . . I'm certain this Jubilee of yours will be an all-time, leg-lifting dog. On the other hand I'm a professional journalist who can change his opinion according to his purse. I'm here to give my readers a taste of forthcoming delights.

Garrick   You can hear my 'Ode to Shakespeare'.

Dibdin   My 'Dawn Serenade', sung by Mrs Garrick herself would be better.

Dr Arne   I've heard it and I have to say I enjoyed a peace I never thought possible, but then I woke up with a feeling I'd been asleep for twenty years.

Grimes *enters upstage centre pushing a small, portable piano.*

Garrick   'To what blest genius of the isle . . .'

Garrick *continues as* **Dr Arne** *plays and* **Dibdin** *accompanies* **Mrs Garrick** *singing 'Dawn Serenade' whilst* **Steevens** *takes notes and the light fades out.*

Scene Twelve

Spot up on **Mrs Garrick**, *dressed for a journey, seated on her luggage, waiting for a coach and idly tap-dancing from a seated position.*

Mrs Garrick That might be true, but why am I waiting for a coach to take me to Stratford? I've been to Paris, Vienna, Rome and now I'm going to *Stratford*! . . . after eating a piece of stale pie he had a stale vision. Now nothing will stop him putting on the Jubilee. That's the story so far, in case anyone hasn't been paying attention . . . (*Her feet tap furiously.*) I should've put my foot down like I'm doing now . . . (*Her tapping rhythms change.*) . . . do I still love him as I swear I do? . . . Once I said 'I'd die for you and you for me, and if you don't believe it, kill me or I'll kill you' . . . is it still true? . . . Yes, though we've been together years, it's still like those honey months after marriage . . . I remember sitting drinking hot chocolate and he said something . . . it doesn't matter what . . . his voice so charmed me I put down my cup and stared . . . his eyes seemed brighter than the sun and it was more than I could bear . . . now one smile can still relieve my sad heart, one hard look can still close it.

Garrick *enters carrying luggage and sits on it like* **Mrs Garrick**.

Garrick Where's the coach? What're you doing, my dear?

Mrs Garrick Talking to myself, thinking on my feet. I was wondering, is true love a practical proposition? What does the world get out of it when lovers like us exist in a world of our own? . . . You once said, the most difficult thing to show on stage is happiness . . . particularly a happy couple, happy in each other.

Garrick It's hard to show with mere words. I've tried to do it with looks, half-turns of the head, hands touching and forming shapes in the air. But the audience is too far away. Perhaps I should've tried sounds.

*They tap softly in perfect harmony with each other and smile. They
stop as a cloud passes overheard and the lights dim slightly.* **Mrs
Garrick** *looks up and shivers.*

Mrs Garrick   The leaves turn brown. Autumn winds,
autumn clouds up there, Davey.

Garrick *looks up.*

Garrick   Just one.

Mrs Garrick   That's all it takes. If the rains come, they
won't be life-giving for us. And September is a rainy month.

Garrick   Not this September. I've consulted Madame Le
Brand, the foremost weather woman in London. She
consulted the spirit world, crystal ball, chicken entrails. The
ball stayed clear and the entrails didn't turn mushy, which
according to all signs and precognitive omens means rain
will be a little late this year.

*There is the sound of a stagecoach and a horn being blown. A life-size
cut-out of a stagecoach and horses is trotted on stage right, carried by a
driver,* **McGurk**, **Grimes** *and* **George Garrick**.

McGurk   All aboard, ladies and gents!

Garrick *and* **Mrs Garrick** *pick up their luggage to join*
George *and* **Grimes** *round the back of the cut-out coach.*

McGurk   Oysters McGurk at your service. I hope yous
come equipped . . . (*He holds up a blunderbuss.*) We're
journeying to dangerous parts. There be dragons, robbers,
brigands and footpads lurking in remote rural roads. I've
high tales o' Baboon Dooley, and Goo-Goo Jim and the
Slaughterhouse Gang. You'll meet most of 'em lining the
roadside, hanging like rotten fruit. Hanging's a fine thing all
round, everyone cheers, eh?

Grimes   Everyone except the criminal.

McGurk   They cheer most of all. Hangings weed out the
weak and incompetent – that means anyone who gets
caught. A hanged man can't tell no secrets. Wholesale

hanging improves the criminal breed. No piss-a-beds left who'll turn white-livered and inform, squeal and betray the rest.

Garrick   We're ready, driver!

Grimes   Crack the whip, McGurk. The sooner we get there, the sooner we'll get back!

There is the sound of a whip cracking and the coach speeds off stage right. After a moment there is a shout.

George Garrick's Voice   McGurk, you're going the wrong way!

McGurk's Voice   What?!

Grimes's Voice   McGurk, you're about as useful as a glass eye at a keyhole!

There is the sound of the coach turning round and it re-enters stage right to trot across the stage.

McGurk   Let's make it cheery, now . . . everybody sing . . . we're Stratford bound!

All (*singing*) 'Oh yes, we're Stratford bound / We have no time, no time, to hang around / No, you won't find us in lost and found / Don't look round / Because we're Stratford, you know, we're Stratford, because we're Stratford bound!'

The cut-out coach exits stage left to the sound of their singing. As the lights fade down, there is a sudden thunderclap and it begins to rain.

Act Two

Scene One

A partly built wooden rotunda, with scaffolding, rope, ladders and building equipment. A broad band of blue silk representing the River Avon stretches upstage. Behind it is the outline of a row of willow trees. The rotunda has a raised round wooden floor with steps. There is a ramp with two planks on the top, connecting it to the raised wooden floor. **Amos Ackers** *trundles a wheelbarrow up the ramp and across the planks to the rotunda floor, whilst* **Ted Ackers** *hammers in some nails up in the scaffolding.*

Amos Ackers   What're we building, Ted?

Ted Ackers   A rotunda. It's for dancing.

Amos Ackers   What do we know about rotundas, Ted?

Ted Ackers   Nothing, Amos, but it's better than looking after sheep.

Amos Ackers   They swore they weren't coming here, building their rotundas.

Ted Ackers   People lie.

Amos Ackers   Sheep don't, unless the one in front of them does it first. I miss them.

Ted Ackers   What about the fluke and foot-rot, Amos? The stale blood, stinkin' gunk, dead flesh and live maggots gnawing skin from bones?

Amos Ackers   You have to take the rough with the smooth with sheep.

Ted Ackers   I miss them too. I hear them baa-baa-baaing in the night.

Amos Ackers   So why're we helping foreigners, Ted?

Ted Ackers   It bites in the mind but we need the money.
We always need the money. It's no fun being poor. You feel
like you're always falling.

Ted Ackers *jumps off the scaffolding whilst clinging to the pulley
rope.* **Amos Ackers**, *holding on to the other end, gets pulled up on
to the scaffolding. The brothers have changed places.*

Amos Ackers   I tell you, Ted, the greatest misery that
can befall a man is to be poor. It makes men desperate
enough to work without joy, live without principle and
abandon their sheep.

Ted Ackers   Even dead we'll be marked. The poor in
paradise have smaller wings and dimmer halos.

Garrick *enters briskly downstage left near the ramp.* **Amos** *slides
down from the scaffolding.*

Garrick   Gather round, men. I can see you're doing your
best. But I want more than your best.

Ted Ackers   How can you ever do more than your best?

Garrick   You're giving me ninety nine percent, but I'm
greedy, I need a hundred and five percent to be ready for
the opening night. Souvenir ribbons have to be sewn and
commemorative medals struck. Where's the place for
fireworks? Master Domico Angelo will be here today . . . (*He
looks upstage.*) And what do we do with that river? And those
willows'll have to go!

The line of willows upstage immediately sink from view. **Sharp**
enters, stage right.

Sharp   I smell wood! Just give me the chance to buy it, sir.
Is it mulberry? No matter. Mulberry, oak, ash, elm or
willow, it's all one to me. Like the alchemists of old, I turn
all wood into mulberry and turn a profit. Oh, the authentic
Shakespearean trinkets I can carve from those trees. I'll pay
top money. I never say 'Woodman, spare that tree'. Sharp's
the name. Tom Sharp, who's never knowingly
undercharged.

He exits stage right.

Garrick   I've no idea who that man was, but he has the kind of ginger to make this Jubilee a success. Brothers Ackers, there're no spear carriers here. I'll be with you every step of the way. I know you usually work at a slower tempo. I've played all kinds of peasants, servants, yokels and halfwits, and I learnt all the suitable idiot proverbs . . . 'He digs deepest who digs deep' . . . 'No leg is too short to reach the ground' . . . 'Don't wipe your arse with a hedgehog'.

Ted Ackers   'It's the oldest fox who lives the longest' . . . 'The bottom step is always the lowest' . . . 'Never play leapfrog with a unicorn'.

Amos Ackers   'Hang a cowpat on the wall / And the rain will surely fall. / Hang a cowpat on the roof / And the rain will stay aloof.'

Ted *and* **Amos Ackers** *have gone into their 'country yokel' mode.*

Ted Ackers }
Amos Ackers }   Arrr . . . Arrr, squire.

Garrick   'Arrr . . . Arrr' brings back memories. Abel Drugger was one of my most famous roles. 'Arrr . . . Arrr' were the most overworked words in my yokel repertoire . . . Now, let's raise our game, get the balloon airborne, see the piecrust rise. It's curtain up, a time for glory!

Galvanised by **Garrick**'*s speech,* **Ted Ackers** *picks up a flimsy wooden door stage right, whilst* **Amos Ackers** *takes a mouthful of nails and starts hammering them, one by one, into a post.* **Garrick** *lifts off the two planks bridging the top of the ramp and the floor of the rotunda as* **Mrs Garrick** *enters stage right, carrying bundles of stage costumes, whilst* **Ted Ackers**, *holding the flimsy door in front of him, goes carefully up the ramp.*

Garrick   I've just given them my inspiring opening night speech. Went down well, didn't it, Ted or is it Amos?

He slaps **Amos Ackers** *on the back, not realising he has a mouthful of nails.* **Amos** *gasps, clutches his throat to prevent himself* *swallowing them. He staggers about, spitting out the nails as* **Ted Ackers** *reaches the top of the ramp, holding the flimsy door in front of him. Not seeing where he is going, he steps out confidently, thinking the planks are still there. There is a short, frightened cry as he crashes to the ground, falling straight through the flimsy door.*

George Garrick *enters stage left with three small boys,* **Bill**, **Jack** *and* **Jimmy**. *They look curiously at* **Ted Ackers** *struggling to extract himself from the smashed door.*

George Garrick   Careful with that equipment, you're liable for all breakages. David, I've got the choirboys to audition for the 'Dawn Serenade'.

Garrick   Are you clean, bright, presentable? Can you sing? Eva, show them the nymph costumes.

Jimmy   Tripes and trullibubs, hold your horses and your dogs, Mister. How much're we being paid?

Garrick   Paid? I thought you'd do it as a service to Stratford.

Bill   Jeekers! What's this twiddle-pooping town to us, matey?!

Jack   A guinea a time's our performing fee.

Mrs Garrick   What do you boys need money for?

Bill   Gin.

Jack   And we're saving.

Garrick   What're you saving for?

Jimmy   Women.

George Garrick   Just sing, boys, sing!

Bill   We don't know this addle-pated 'Dawn Serenade'.

Mrs Garrick   Then sing something you do know.

The boys climb up on to the rotunda to sing with lovely, pure, unbroken voices.

Bill ⎱ (*singing*) 'We have a tenement to let/We hope
Jack ⎰ to please you all/And if you'd know the name
Jimmy ⎰ of it / It is called Nookie Hall/Nookie Hall,
Nookie Hall / It's seated in a pleasant vale / Beneath a
rising hill / This tenement is to be let / If you can pay the
bill / Pay the bill, pay the bill . . .'

Garrick   Stop!

Jimmy   There're four more verses of unwashed bawdy.

Mrs Garrick   I can imagine!

Jack   Do we get the job, Squinty? One guinea a throw.

Garrick   Let's get to know each other before we talk
money. Have you boys seen my famous peacock and
turkey?

Garrick *does a dazzling mime of a proud peacock and gobbling
turkey. The boys look on, stony-faced.*

Bill   It's still a guinea a throw.

George Garrick   David, there's no one else as good.

Jimmy   You're right there . . . guineas in advance,
Blubber-cheeks.

Garrick   Done.

The boys exit excitedly stage left.

George Garrick   Wild rogues, imps of Satan.

Garrick   I thought country folk were all natural and
innocent. I must change the way I play them in future.

Mrs Garrick   What do we do with these stage costumes,
David?

Garrick   I want a parade through Stratford with our
guests dressed as various Shakespearean characters . . . (*He
picks up a costume.*) I can see the Duke of Dorset with his gouty
foot as Lear. (*He throws the Lear costume over his shoulders and imitates
Dorset playing King Lear.*) 'You heavens, give me that patience I

need / You see me here, you gods, a poor old man. As full of grief as age; wretched in both! . . .' (*He limps on his gouty leg.*) Ahh, oooh, ahh! . . . 'And let not woman's weapons water drops / Strain my man's cheeks!' . . . Ahh, ooh, ahh' . . . (*He drapes a Roman toga over his shoulders.*) And what of Master Steevens as Cassius . . . (*He imitates* **Steevens**, *playing Cassius.*) 'Why, man, Garrick, doth bestride the narrow world / Like a colossus and we petty men / Walk under his huge legs and peer about' . . .

George Garrick   We should charge a fee for using the costumes.

Mrs Garrick   They'll come back in tatters. The rich have no respect for other people's property.

Garrick   We must engender a spirit of community, even if it's expensive. We'll have horse races, fireworks, singing, dancing, glees, a masquerade and parade through the street, culminating in the great Ode.

Mrs Garrick   Any Shakespeare?

Garrick   What?

George Garrick   Will we be producing a Shakespeare play?

Garrick   No.

George Garrick   Thank God.

Garrick   We must treat our visitors gently. Why traipse off to the Warwickshire wilds to see Shakespeare in a forgotten country town in the middle of nowhere? Everybody who's anybody's been seeing him in comfort for years, in town. We have to give them something different.

Mrs Garrick   Yes, they want to be entertained.

Lights out.

Scene Two

Night. **Dr Arne**, **Dibdin** *and* **Mrs Ross** *enter in a line stage left led by* **Steevens**. *They carry lanterns and are trying to find their way in the dark.*

Steevens   It's an outrage. We paid the stagecoach to deposit us at the White Hart Inn in the centre of Stratford.

Mrs Ross   Perhaps this is the centre of Stratford. I'm glad I got my girls to come by day coach.

An owl hoots.

Steevens   What was that?

Dibdin   A barn owl.

Dr Arne   No, that's a bay owl, pretending to be a barn.

Mrs Ross   How can you tell the difference?

Dr Arne   You can't.

Dibdin   I was right, then.

Dr Arne   Dibdin, I've seen oranges bigger than your head.

Steevens   What're we doing, lost out here in the stars?

Dibdin   Good title for a song, 'What're We Doing?'

Dr Arne   Thank you, Dibdin, and now you can pull the chain.

Mrs Ross   It's all your fault, Mr Steevens. The driver took offence at your remarks about Stratford.

Steevens   What remarks?

Mrs Ross   Like, 'Stratford is a cemetery with lights'. And 'There're some nice walks out of Stratford. Any walk is a nice walk out of Stratford.'

Dibdin And what about 'They flattened the whole town during the Civil War and did one guinea's worth of damage.'

Steevens I've nothing against Stratford, I just prefer to spend one day in it instead of three. Why didn't Garrick hold the Jubilee within easy walking distance at the Globe, Bankside?

Mrs Ross Perhaps he wanted to create difficulties for us so we'd enjoy it more.

Dibdin The public don't want difficulties. They want smooth swallows. The easier the entertainment is to digest, the more they like it. That's why I always give the customers what they like.

Dr Arne Only prostitutes give their customers what they like. An artist doesn't ask the public what it likes. He determines it.

Steevens I can't listen to arty credos, I'm ankle deep in cow shit.

John Ange *enters stage right. When he sees the others, he quickly sticks a long straw in his mouth.*

Ange Arrr, eee, arrr, be you folk up a creek without the proverbial paddle?

Mrs Ross And are you the proverbial village idiot?

Ange Not at the moment, Missus, we take it in turns . . . (*He holds out his hand.*) If I'd've known you weren't going to pay me fer talking, I wouldn't've said anything.

Dr Arne Sorry, we forgot we were in Stratford.

Steevens Can you tell us the way to the White Hart Inn?

Ange Arrr, well now, that depends from where you start from, squire. If it's from Pebworth, you go through Grafton and turn left at Marston. But if you start from Papist

Wickford, you go through Broom and Bidford via Haunted Hillborough.

Dibdin   How do you get to the White Hart Inn from *here*?

Ange   From here? Ah, I've never done that.

Steevens   You're a complete fool.

Ange   That's as may be, but I'm not lost.

Mrs Ross   If you can't tell us the way, can you tell us the time?

Ange   Arrr, to be sure.

Dr Arne   What is it, man?

Ange   You can't get it free, sir. Festival time costs money.

Mrs Ross   We pay for the time?

Ange   It's valuable, specially if you haven't got it. A shilling and cheap at the price.

Dibdin   A shilling!

Ange   Jubilee prices, sir. Jubilee prices.

Steevens *angrily gives him a coin.*

Steevens   Now, what's the time?

Ange   Thankee kindly, kind sir . . . (*He glances quickly at his watch.*) . . . it's ten o'clock.

Mrs Ross   So, it's exactly ten o'clock?

Ange   Well now, 't'aint *exactly* ten o'clock. It's some minutes past exactly ten o'clock.

Steevens   How many minutes past?

Ange   Arrr now, minutes'll cost you extra. Jubilee prices, sir! Jubilee prices!

Dr Arne *and* **Dibdin** *hold* **Steevens** *back as he tries to throttle* **Ange**, *who makes a hurried exit, stage left.*

Dr Arne   This is what you get for trying to bring culture to the masses. Shakespeare is for those who can appreciate him, not an excuse to charge Jubilee prices.

Steevens   Don't forget we're in enemy territory, surrounded by farmers! – skinflints who'd drain ponds, lakes and rivers dry if they could sell the mud at the bottom for a profit; whose fingers've grown into talons from grasping so long and hard; who see ducks flying over their land as trespassers; who'd carry God to market if they could get a good price for him.

Mrs Ross   And we're still lost.

A comet, with a long fiery tail, shoots across the night sky.

Dibdin   A light sent by the God of Music to show us the way.

Dr Arne   Halley's Comet. It appears once every seventy-five years . . . it's all so vast, there must be people on other planets.

Dibdin   So why don't they contact us?

Dr Arne   Would you?

Steevens   Aren't comets supposed to be omens of coming disasters?

Mrs Ross   Follow it! It probably knows the way to the White Hart.

They exit quickly in the same direction as the comet.

Scene Three

The garden of **Hunt**'s *house, Stratford. Halley's Comet arcs across the night sky above them as* **Mrs Garrick** *stands by a table and examines the insides of a chicken, pine cones and other herbs. She is watched anxiously by* **Garrick** *and* **George Garrick**.

George Garrick   Halley's Comet. A bad omen, Davey.

Garrick   I don't believe in such superstitions. What's it to be, Eva, wet, dry, cold, hot, calm or stormy?

Mrs Garrick   I'm not an expert like Madame Le Brand but according to this chicken gizzard the weather's going to be unsettled for the rest of the week. The pine cones're half open, which means it'll be warm. On the other hand, you could consider them half closed, which means it would be cold. Half open, or half closed, it depends on how you interpret the mystic signs.

Garrick   In other words, you don't know?

Mrs Garrick   That's right.

George Garrick   My knee knows. I've been getting signals from my left knee all day . . . here! Here! (*He hits his left knee.*) . . . The one I smashed getting you out of that hole in the ice.

Garrick   George rescued me when we were boys sledging on a pond outside Lichfield and I was going under.

Mrs Garrick   I don't know that story.

George Garrick   It's not important. What is important is you're going under again, Davey, unless I pull you out. When my gammy knee speaks, I listen. It says it's going to rain.

Mrs Garrick   Listen to his knee, his knee, Davey.

George Garrick   My knee and that Comet predict a disaster. Go back to London, Davey.

Mrs Garrick   Surely it's too late for that? What could we say?

George Garrick   Say it was my fault. Nothing was ready when you got here. You put me in charge and the whole thing was mismanaged from the start. I'll back up your story. The public'll be furious; less so when we refund their money. It'll be a five-day wonder but forgotten by the end of your next Covent Garden Season. It'll be put down to me.

Garrick   Did you know I had such a brother, Eva?

Mrs Garrick   I always knew.

Garrick *puts his arm round* **George***'s shoulders.*

Garrick   I love you for it but I say no, George. When I
form some plan or course of action, I find a voice inside me
I can't account for. I let the voice lie unheard. It may pass,
but if it doesn't, I listen and yield. Don't ask me to describe
it, I can't. It's too simple to describe; it's like a seed in the
soul. It grows, drowning out reason. I have that roaring
voice in me now, telling me I must lead this Jubilee for
Shakespeare's sake. Abuse from the whole world couldn't
make me ignore or change it. By the time I'm finished, even
the dogs will believe I'm right.

The light from Halley's Comet fades out to the sound of applause.

Scene Four

The interior of the White Hart Inn. The innkeeper, **John Payton***,
serves drinks to* **Hunt***,* **Wheeler***,* **Rev. Jago***,* **Grimes***,*
Lydia *and* **Charmaine** *who have been watching Halley's Comet
off left and applauding as it finally dies away.*

Lydia   It was beautiful.

Wheeler   Not as beautiful as you, my dear. Halley's
Comet lit up but a small patch of darkness. Your beauty
lights up the whole night sky!

They cross to the bar where **Grimes** *joins them.*

Hunt   How goes it, Mr Grimes?

Grimes   Oh, I could tell you things but me throat's gone
dry. I'm suffering from bottle fatigue, gents.

Hunt   More beer, Mr Payton.

Payton *hands them six tankards.*

Payton   Two guineas, sir.

Hunt   Two guineas for six pints!

Payton   Jubilee prices.

Rev. Jago   But we're natives.

Payton   Natives or foreigners it's Jubilee prices. All're equal in the White Hart.

Hunt *pays him and they drink.*

Grimes   In my opinion, gents, the good ship Jubilee is heading for trouble. The one I'm sorry for is Master David. He's a prince amongst men and almost a decent actor. A disaster could stain his name for ever. Look at me. I was a rising comedy actor as Milo O'Casey.

Rev. Jago   I never go to the theatre, a nest of thieves, whores and Papists.

Grimes   I played Dublin and told an Irish joke. Paddy O'Flynn's wife asked what he'd do if he came home one night and found her in bed with another man. O'Flynn said, 'I'd shoot his guide dog.' There were a lot of O'Flynns in the audience and I was lucky to get out alive. It was never the same again.

Wheeler   You think it's that way with the Jubilee?

Rev. Jago   We've backed the wrong horse! The very title 'Jubilee' sounds Papist, if not down right Jewish. Who's interested in this Shakespeare, who's heard of this Shakespeare, outside a stew of London wits? We grow the best turnips in England. We could've had a Turnip Jubilee, celebrating glorious Stratford turnips. It would've been a winner!

Mrs Ross, **Dibdin**, **Dr Arne** *and* **Steevens** *enter, the worse for wear, upstage centre.*

Lydia   Mrs Ross, you finally came.

Mrs Ross   Save that remark for your customers, Lydia.

Steevens How dare the coach company treat the best critic in England like this?

Hunt I always thought critics were small, rodent-like creatures with padlocked ears and blinkers.

Payton *brings them drinks.*

Grimes Strong liquor makes me maudlin. Let's drink to a disaster – the Jubilee!

Steevens How can it be a disaster? I haven't written about it yet.

Grimes It's ended before it's begun, but I've enjoyed a good life. I've had it all, from the smile to the grin, from the grin to the chuckle, from the chuckle to the laugh, from the laugh to the roar, from the roar to the boffo. What more can a man ask?

Mrs Ross First night nerves, Grimes. Take a grip. Did you bring the costumes?

Grimes *indicates the costumes.*

Mrs Ross Lydia, Charmaine, we haven't much time. I promised Lord Dorset we'd put on a show for him tonight in honour of the Bard. A little prologue before the Jubilee proper. We'll change in our rooms.

Payton Jubilee prices, Mrs Ross but worth every half-penny now I've named them after Shakespeare's plays. Mrs Ross you'll have the *As You Like It* suite . . . (*The men chortle.*) Lydia and Charmaine share the *Twelfth Night or What You Will* deluxe double . . . (*The men cheer.*) . . . and I'm saving the *Much Ado About Nothing* three-room special for Lord Dorset.

Lydia, **Charmaine** *and* **Mrs Ross** *scoop up the costumes and go up the stairs.*

Dibdin I think they may need some help. I have an instinct for fashion.

He speeds up after them.

Dr Arne   Where're our rooms, innkeeper? I don't care what they're called, *A Comedy of Errors*.

Steevens   Or *Love's Labours Lost.* Just as long as I have a room with a view.

Payton   You have. Your table's by the window, there. That's the advantage of booking. If you hadn't booked in advance, you'd've ended up in the chicken coop with the others.

Dr Arne   You mean we sleep on tables?

Payton   On or under, it makes no odds to me.

Steevens   And you're charging . . . ?

Payton   You've got it, gents, Jubilee prices! I have to make it now or for ever hold my peace. That's why my breeches have one-way pockets for the duration.

Lord Dorset *hobbles in.*

Lord Dorset   Where're the bawds, the brawny-bummed bawds?! I've just had a splendid day at the races. Now I want to do some more hard riding. I'm supposed to be entertained by Mrs Ross and her ladies.

Payton   They're upstairs, changing, Your Lordship. Your room's ready.

Steevens   You get a room and we get hard tables.

Lord Dorset   I've found if you're filthy rich, you can always get a room, with a bath . . . drinks all round.

Grimes   Finest words in the English language . . . angels love comedy.

Dr Arne   What?

Grimes   I'm convinced if there are really angels, they love comedy. Our whining, whingeing, snivelling prayers must drive them mad. It's our laughter they want, the pratfalls, the dropped pants, the pie in the face, the ferret down the trousers. See how they clap their wings and shake with angelic laughter.

Dibdin *comes back down the stairs.*

Rev. Jago   Time for me to go. I confess, I don't like William Shakespeare. By the end of one of his speeches, I've forgotten the beginning. What about you, Hunt? Do you really think he's good?

Hunt   I don't know. I didn't become an owner of property and a town councillor by backing my own judgement. I follow the crowd. I think Shakespeare's good because he sounds good but I only know he's good if other people say he is. The more people say he's good, the more certain I become. If this Jubilee's a success, everyone will say he's the best. Then I'll know he is for sure.

Rev. Jago   Do you like him, Wheeler?

Wheeler   Not as much as I like compliments, or my own way, or roast beef with gravy, or treacle pudding or this old scarf, or my dog, Scruff. But I like him well enough.

Payton   Gentlemen, in keeping with our policy of providing popular English entertainment, the White Hart Inn gives you the latest in vice, drunkenness and bawdy . . . Maestros, an intro to *Cleo and Tony* if you please!

Lights dim as **Dibdin** *and* **Dr Arne** *sit down at the piano and play suitable Oriental-sounding music. Spot up on the top of the stairs as* **Mrs Ross** *appears, dressed as Cleopatra in a robe too big for her. She is cheered. There are even bigger cheers as* **Lydia** *and* **Charmaine** *appear behind her as two half-naked handmaidens, one carrying a basket, the other a crown.* **Mrs Ross** *comes elegantly down the stairs, only to trip half-way down, and skid down the last few steps on her bottom.*

Mrs Ross   Damnable dress! . . . (*She picks herself up with dignity.*) But still every bloody inch a queen . . . 'Put on my crown; I have / Immortal longings in me' . . . (*She hitches up* *her dress, which keeps slipping, and looks lecherously at the men.*) 'The juice of Egypt's grape shall moist this lip' . . .

Grimes   Me too, me too!

Mrs Ross   'Come then and take the last warmth of my lips' . . .   (**Grimes** *rushes forward to kiss her but she flattens him.*) Not you, sonny . . . 'Farewell, kind Charmian; Iras, long farewell.'

She kisses **Charmaine** *and then* **Lydia** *who swoons, making sure her dress rucks up, exposing herself as she falls in a heap. The men applaud.*

Rev. Jago   I didn't know Shakespeare was like this?

Wheeler   Educational but dirty with it.

Mrs Ross   'Methinks I hear Antony call; I see him raise himself' . . .

Steevens   I'm raised.

Dibdin   Me too.

Dr Arne   I could have a very normal sex life if it wasn't for my wife.

Mrs Ross   'To praise my noble act; I hear him mock / The luck of Caesar . . . husband I come.'

Lord Dorset   Gad! . . . I say she's more to be petted than censured.

Mrs Ross   'I am fire and air; my other elements / I give to baser life – So – have you done?'

Lord Dorset   Done! We haven't even started yet.

Mrs Ross   'This proves me base; / If she first meet the curled Antony . . . / Come thou mortal wretch. . .' The asp, the asp, girl!

Charmaine *takes a small rubber snake out of her basket.*

Charmaine   It's the asp.

As the rubber snake jumps into the air **Mrs Ross** *catches it.*

Mrs Ross   'Poor venomous fool . . . / Be angry and despatch.'

She applies the snake to her breast but she drops it and it falls down inside her gown.

Charmaine   The asp! . . . The asp!

Mrs Ross   I know it's the asp!

She jumps up and wriggles. **Charmaine** *tries to help.* **Lydia** *starts to get up but* **Charmaine** *pushes her down.*

Charmaine   You're unconscious.

Mrs Ross   Ahh, ooh . . . where is it?

Grimes   Let me give a helping hand.

Mrs Ross   Keep your hands to yourself, laddie!

Lord Dorset   Careful where it creeps into, madam.

Steevens   Naughty little asp.

Dibdin *and* **Dr Arne** *play furiously.*

Wheeler   Jago, is something wrong with your peepers? They're sticking out of your head like prawn eyes.

Mrs Ross *jumps up and down, trying to get the snake to fall out of her gown.*

Mrs Ross   O eastern star! . . . the asp! . . . the asp!

Grimes   What a routine.

Mrs Ross *stops jumping as the rubber snake drops out of her gown. She jumps on it with both her feet.*

Mrs Ross   Peace, peace! . . . give me another asp, Charmaine.

Charmaine *takes out another asp and throws it across to* **Mrs Ross**.

Hunt   That's two asps in one basket.

Mrs Ross *applies the asp to her arm.*

Mrs Ross   'As sweet as balm, as soft as air, as gentle . . . /
O Antony . . .'

As she collapses spectacularly, she throws the snake, **Charmaine**
catches it and suggestively pushes it between her breasts.

Charmaine   'O, come apace, dispatch: I partly feel
thee. . .'

Lord Dorset   Whoo there, dobbin! Obscenity doesn't
bother me provided it's in good taste.

Charmaine *collapses seductively, making sure she exposes as much
of herself as possible.*

Charmaine   Ah, sailor!

She lies still. **Dr Arne** *and* **Dibdin** *play final chords and the others
roar their approval. They rush over to the women to congratulate them.*

Rev. Jago   It's a miracle. Now I understand why we're
holding this Jubilee. I used to think miracles were hailstones
on Mid-Summer Eve, the sun coming out at night, or angels
dancing on a pin. But most miracles are run-of-the-mill
affairs, mild winds turning into gales, orchards from one
cherry stone, sunsets and dawns, me seeing Shakespeare's a
great writer!

Lights out.

Scene Five

Lights up. **Garrick**'s *bedroom. Early morning.* **Mrs Garrick** *is
asleep in the bed, as* **Garrick** *in his nightgown does some exercises
and breathes deeply.*

Mrs Garrick   David?

Garrick   This country air makes a man feel good. I was up at six a.m., the crack of dawn, took a brisk walk to the privy and was back in bed by six five.

Mrs Garrick   You're nervous.

Garrick   I've staked my reputation on this Jubilee. Have I let my passion for Shakespeare blind me? Is he the greatest poet this island has known? Or does he just provide me with good parts? What do you think, Eva?

Mrs Garrick   I don't think, I feel.

Garrick   Do you feel William Shakespeare is the poet I feel he is?

Mrs Garrick   *You* feel he is and that's what's important! Passion is all.

Garrick   I sway but his words cast a spell I can't break . . . 'In sooth, I know not why I am so sad' . . . 'O! now for ever/Farewell the tranquil mind; farewell content! / Farewell the plumèd troop and the big wars.'

Mrs Garrick   You're going to bring the dead to life, Davey, breathe on his bones and make them dance again.

He kisses her. There is a knock on the door, upstage centre.

Garrick   Who's there?

Grimes's Voice   A nobody.

Mrs Garrick *slips out of bed and goes into the bathroom stage left.*

Garrick   Nobody can come in.

Grimes *enters with shaving equipment on a small trolley.* **Grimes** *has a terrible hangover and he winces every time the trolley rattles.* **Garrick** *sits for his morning shave.*

Garrick   You had a good evening.

Grimes *puts a towel round* **Garrick**'s *neck.*

Grimes   I went from tavern to tavern, telling the world what a sparkling success the Jubilee was going to be.

He lathers **Garrick**'s *chin.*

Garrick   You mean you went around spreading gloom and despondency. Some men turn whole landscapes into perpetual winters.

Grimes   That's why they call me 'Shine' or 'Sunshine Grimes'. I know the Jubilee will be a success but I can't stop painting shadows on the wall. I have a pessimistic disposition.

He picks up the cut-throat razor with trembling hands.

Garrick   Are you up to shaving me this morning?

Grimes   I resent that, Master Davey. You've forgotten my famous balloon-shaving routine. I'd lather 'em and then shave six balloons in a row without bursting them.

Garrick   Oh yes, great act. When I first saw it I heard laughter at the very back of the theatre. I naturally assumed someone was telling jokes back there.

Grimes   I earned more than enough to keep me alive even if I died on my feet every night.

At that moment there is a volley of cannons. **Grimes** *jumps into the air in fright, cutting* **Garrick**'s *cheek.*

Garrick   I'm bleeding!

Grimes *holds his head as* **Garrick** *sticks a tiny piece of paper over the cut.*

Grimes   Sorry about that, Master Davey. It won't happen again. The balloons. Remember the balloons.

Garrick *sits warily and* **Grimes** *resumes shaving him.*

Garrick   That was a volley of cannons to open the Jubilee. I hope they were firing in the right direction.

Grimes   You mean on Stratford?

Garrick   It's too early for jokes.

Grimes   It's never too early or too late. Have you heard? Three footpads staged a smash and grab in Edinburgh and got caught when they went back for the brick.

As **Garrick** *laughs, despite himself, there is a loud pealing of church bells.* **Grimes** *reacts violently again.* **Garrick** *yells as he is nicked on the other cheek.*

Garrick   I'm bleeding again!

He tears off another tiny piece of paper and sticks it on the new cut. The church bells stop pealing.

Grimes   What's going on?

Garrick   Death by a thousand cuts. The bells were part of the Jubilee opening.

Grimes   Sit, Master Davey. I'm a pro. This is a great moment for you. You and you alone will change the English theatre for all time. You must look your best.

He pushes **Garrick** *back into the chair and resumes shaving him with extreme care. But even as his razor touches* **Garrick***, the Band of the Warwickshire Militia blast out a military march outside.* **Garrick** *yells and clasps his chin. This time* **Grimes** *hands him the tiny piece of paper to slap on his latest cut.*

Garrick   No more shaving.

Grimes   You're receiving the freedom of Stratford this morning, Master Davey. You can't go unshaven. I'll close the window curtains. You have to admire my persistence, Master Davey.

Garrick   There's nothing I admire about you, Grimes.

Grimes *crosses to close the window curtains but the band stops.*

Grimes   Perfect silence. It reminds me of Macklin when he played Richard III and Richard lost. But that performance had a happy ending. The curtain finally came down.

He has coaxed **Garrick** *back into the chair and resumes shaving.
They don't notice* **Dibdin** *creeping in upstage centre with the small
boys choir of* **Bill**, **Jack** *and* **Jimmy**, *dressed as nymphs.* **Dibdin**
lines them up and gives a signal.

Bill
Jack $\Big\}$ (*singing*) 'Let beauty with the sun arise. . .'
Jimmy

Grimes *jumps back in fright.* **Garrick** *yells and stanches another
cut on his face as* **Mrs Garrick** *rushes out of the bathroom. Lights
out with the choir still singing.*

Scene Six

Lights up on a room in the Stratford Town Hall. **George
Garrick**, **Wheeler**, **Rev. Jago**, **Lord Dorset**, **Dibdin**,
Dr Arne, **Steevens**, **Mrs Ross**, **Lydia** *and* **Charmaine**
are waiting.

Lord Dorset   My foot's throbbing, sir, throbbing,
throbbing fit to be tied. Let's get on with it!

Hunt   We can't without Mr Garrick, my lord.

Trumpets sound.

Wheeler   Good, he's here.

The respectful silence is broken by a familiar braying laugh as **James
Boswell** *enters stage right.*

Boswell   Have I missed anything? I'm paying Jubilee
prices.

Rev. Jago   No, Mr Garrick hasn't arrived yet.

Boswell   I saw him being driven back to London, ha-ha-
ha! . . . My Lord Dorset, how are you?

Lord Dorset   Keep away from my foot, sir!

Boswell   George, we haven't met since . . .

George Garrick   No, not since.

Mrs Ross   Yes, not since.

Boswell   I grow more bemused as I grow older. I was in London last week seeking medical advice. A touch of the brush, Mrs Ross. Now I'm as clean as a whistle, tell the girls. And I was collaborating with Doctor Johnson on a biblical epic. He thinks it needs some laughs so he's hired a friend. I'd rather have a 'name' but I bowed to his judgement as always . . . anyway, one minute I was in London, the next I was in Gretna Green in a parcel.

Mrs Ross   A parcel?

Dr Arne   I've heard of babies being found in handbags, but never a fully grown man in a parcel in Gretna Green.

Boswell   I was wrapped in brown paper, stamped and posted home.

Dibdin   It sounds romantic. Who did it?

Boswell   I suspect me. I'd been drinking.

Mrs Ross   You must've been homesick.

George Garrick   And don't forget going as a parcel is cheaper than taking a stagecoach.

Boswell   True, even drunk, I'm a Scotsman. I could've gone on to Edinburgh, I'd paid the postage, but I wouldn't miss the Jubilee.

Trumpets sound and **Garrick** *and* **Mrs Garrick** *enter solemnly, stage right.* **Mrs Garrick** *is in a dress covered with silver whilst* **Garrick** *looks splendid in a velvet suit, trimmed with gold, and white gloves. The effect is marred by dozens of small pieces of paper all over his face.*

Steevens   I love the jacket, Garrick. So tasteful. But the gloves're out of place.

Garrick   They're Shakespeare's own. Straight from his temple, the first time out of their glass case. These're the gloves that warmed the hands, that held the quill, that wrote the plays, that live for ever.

Mrs Ross   Do you believe some of his spirit is still in those gloves?

Garrick   Yes, just as it's in the fields and hedgerows all around us. Stratford's another Jerusalem where he once walked and talked. His genius inhabits the brute bricks of the town, just as the spirit of the son of God inhabits the holy stones of Israel.

Steevens   And the bits of paper stuck all over your face? Are they inhabited by the spirit of Shakespeare too?

Garrick   No, just Grimes and his balloons.

Hunt   Mr Garrick, as Steward of the Jubilee, Stratford hereby presents you with this medallion and mulberry wand, made from Shakespeare's own tree.

He presents **Garrick** *with a thin wooden wand and a medallion which he drapes round his neck.*

Wheeler   And now Reverend Jago will bestow a blessing on this opening. The floor is yours, Jago, but the roof is ours.

Rev. Jago   Lord God, look down on this holy Jubilee and let the sun shine, that's all we ask. Last night I had a conversion like Paul's on the Damascus road, the one from here to there. Last night I saw for the first time we weren't just celebrating a home-town boy made good. Last night I knew Shakespeare was a touchstone of literary excellence, a poet who made us understand ourselves, a monument to King and country, hearth and home. He moves me to speak in tongues . . . to be or not to be, once more into the breech, this above all to thine own self be true . . . coming from mixed parentage myself, that's good advice . . . what light through yonder window breaks? When the quality of mercy and the barge she sat in, but if music be the food of love, tomorrow and tomorrow, blah, blah, blah, blah.

Garrick *waves his wand and* **Rev. Jago** *stops.*

Garrick Thank you, Reverend Jago and goodnight. I couldn't've put it better myself but I'll try. First the Shakespeare Pageant . . . (*He consults a clipboard.*) . . . Lord Dorset will be appearing as King Lear.

Lord Dorset Ooh, ahh, ooh.

Mrs Garrick Very good Lear acting, My Lord.

Lord Dorset Not acting, madam, my gout's killing me.

Garrick Mrs Ross will be coming as Juliet? You're Juliet?!

Mrs Ross Every inch.

George Garrick But Juliet was sixteen and a virgin.

Mrs Ross Use your imagination.

Garrick My brother George will appear as . . . as what?

George Garrick I couldn't make up my mind between Henry V or Iago, so I'll come as Hamlet.

Garrick James Boswell will appear as a Corsican patriot. What Shakespeare play is that from?

Boswell It's got nothing to do with Shakespeare. I'm promoting my new book, *Travels In Corsica*. I have a few signed copies left. Not at Jubilee prices.

Garrick Mr Steevens is now appearing as Prospero.

Steevens I have my book and magic wand.

He produces a wand.

Garrick As Jubilee Steward I'm the only one allowed a wand!

Steevens On guard . . . (*They duel, using their wands like swords.*) Touché and touchette.

Garrick Didn't we meet in Heidelberg?

Mrs Garrick   David, they have to get dressed.

Garrick *and* **Steevens** *stop fighting.*

Garrick   We'll continue this another time, sir . . . the rest of you know your parts. Now remember, be natural, for life itself is only another pageant, rounded by a deep sleep; a pageant enlivened by love and imagination and threatened by mortality, corruptibility . . .

Dibdin   And rain. It looks like rain.

There is the sound of distant thunder.

Garrick   I forbid it. George, move out!

George Garrick   (*singing*) 'This is the day, a holiday, a holiday / Drive spleen and rancour far away / This is the day, a holiday, a holiday / Drive care and sorrow far away.'

They all exit except **Garrick** *and* **Mrs Garrick**.

Garrick   It won't rain.

Mrs Garrick   No, it won't rain.

They dance together.

Garrick   I'm sure of it.

Mrs Garrick   I'm sure of it.

Garrick   True love . . . is it normal? I mean, true love descends from nowhere but why on us and not two others?

Mrs Garrick   I know friends whisper behind their hands . . . look at those two, they're always so devoted, couldn't they fake it a little and be disappointed in each other once in a while, just for our sakes?

Garrick   I let the people who've never found true love keep saying there's no such thing, if that's what they like.

Mrs Garrick   We need no letters when we're apart. A remembered smile, a half-remembered joke is enough. Anywhere, everywhere is here, my love.

It starts to rain. They continue dancing.

Garrick Is it raining?

Mrs Garrick Yes.

Garrick But I'm still dry.

Mrs Garrick So am I.

Garrick It seems real.

Mrs Garrick It's a stage effect.

There is another clap of thunder.

Garrick That's how we remain dry and can hear each other in the middle of a storm. Otherwise you wouldn't be able to hear me say 'I love you'.

Mrs Garrick And you couldn't hear me answer 'I love you'.

They sing softly and dance despite the rain.

Garrick } (*singing*) 'This is the day, a holiday, a
Mrs Garrick } holiday / Drive spleen and rancour far away / This is the day, a holiday, a holiday/Drive care and sorrow far away.'

Lights fade out.

Scene Seven

*Spot up on **Steevens** downstage centre.*

Steevens The pageant's off, and I'm wet, cold and stinkin'; up to my arse in age-old sewage. Yet I smile, I laugh, I guffaw. The Jubilee's already a disaster and it's hardly started. Like any critic I can't see a belt without hitting below it. I have the compassion of an uncle and the generosity of a money-lender but I talk true . . . let's talk true. Any poltroon whom nature has made weak and idleness kept ignorant can massage his vanity by calling himself a critic. You, out there in the dark, you who are passing through the world in total obscurity, you, yes, you can easily pull yourself out of the quicksands of oblivion by calling yourself one. It's a profession which is respectable, malicious and utterly irrelevant, except to those poor fools who've no opinions of their own. I exult in Garrick's misery. His vanity exceeds my own by some twenty-five miles. How dare he resurrect Shakespeare and try to restore his sleeping reputation? That's my job, the job of a professional. We can kill a poet's fame, so we can restore it when he's safely dead. Like Jesus, we're in the resurrection business full-time. After this Jubilee, Shakespeare's name will slide back with the forgotten dead. If it ever comes to life it'll be because of professional critics like me.

He staggers off stage left unaware he has been watched by **Amos** *and* **Ted Ackers** *who come forward in a spot.*

Amos Ackers   I'm not impressed by educated folk.

Ted Ackers   Wouldn't survive a day in Stratford. It's so tough here, if you're not home by ten o'clock you're declared legally dead.

Amos Ackers   They finally tore down our old street and put up a slum.

Ted Ackers   We know if you want to make a living you have to work for it. If you want to become rich you have to find another way.

Amos Ackers   I've had it hard because I'm not clever. I didn't ask the right questions like, if ignorance is bliss, why aren't there more happy people in the world?

Ted Ackers   Who're we, Amos? What're we, Amos?

Amos Ackers   Comic relief.

Spot out.

Scene Eight

Lights up on the completed rotunda. It is a circular, wooden structure like a bandstand. The **Guests** *are sitting or standing stage right as* **Garrick** *enters in his steward's costume and carrying his ceremonial wand.*

Garrick Ladies and gentlemen, though the pageant was cancelled, the rest of this afternoon's Jubilee entertainment continues unabated.

Grimes *enters and drops a tray.*

Grimes Sorry, sir, I didn't mean to wake the audience.

Garrick They are awake.

Grimes It's hard to tell.

Garrick Did you come out here to embarrass me?

Grimes Somebody has to try.

Garrick Do you think it's easy standing here and commanding an audience?

Grimes No, just brave.

Garrick I suppose you think you could entertain these people? They paid a fortune to get in.

Garrick
Grimes } Jubilee prices!

Grimes *exits to applause.*

Garrick Ladies and Gentlemen, without more ado, although I can do with all the ado I can get, I would like to introduce the world's greatest choir. Unfortunately, I have to introduce Stratford's 'Little Gleesters' . . . (**George Garrick** *hurries on and whispers to* **Garrick**.) I should've said Stratford's 'Little Gleesters' need no introduction. They haven't turned up. Our next performers will certainly add something to the entertainment – at least four minutes.

Lydia *and* **Charmaine** *enter in low-cut dresses.*

Lydia   Thank you. Of all the introductions we've had, yours is the most recent.

Charmaine   We give you 'The Country Girl', specially written by Mr Garrick for the Jubilee.

There is a musical accompaniment led by **Dibdin**.

Lydia   Prithee, tell me Cousin Sue, why do they make so much to-do?

Charmaine   You mean all this clatter? All this noise and chatter?

Lydia   I cannot guess what's the matter.

Charmaine   It's a Jubilee for a poet who is dead.

Lydia   I don't believe what you just said. All this for a dead poet? Oh, no.

Charmaine   Oh, yes, a poet who lived, Lord knows how long ago.

Lydia   It must be for some great man. A prince, an earl or a stale statesman. It can't be for a dead poet – oh, no.

Guests   Oh, yes!

Charmaine   And our dead poet is poor.

Lydia   Are you sure? No one regards a poor poet with awe – oh, no.

Guests   Oh, yes!

Charmaine   Sweet Sue, you're wrong. We celebrate in dance and song. From heart to heart, let joy rebound. See we tread on enchanted ground. A carpet of flowers without a weed. For here sweet Shakespeare lived and breathed.

The audience clap enthusiastically. **Mrs Ross** *hurries to them.*

Mrs Ross   I'm proud of you. You behaved like ladies. You've made the jump from two-penny whores to expensive courtesans. From now on you'll be able to charge Jubilee prices!

Garrick   Now, the happiest announcement of the day. Dinner is being served in the Town Hall.

The **Guests** *thunder out leaving* **Garrick**, **Mrs Garrick** *and* **George Garrick**.

Mrs Garrick   What's wrong, Davey?

Garrick   I think we just died.

George Garrick   Socrates said, 'He who knows the world won't rejoice over his good fortune or be downcast over his bad.'

Mrs Garrick   Socrates was a cantankerous, mean-minded old bigot. I prefer Solomon who told us to kick up our heels in the days of prosperity and shed a tear or two in adversity.

Garrick   You're right, as always, my dear. According to the Venerable Bede, gazelles once grazed on Stratford Green. We must entice them back. It's a challenge but you can never make a true actor despair.

They exit upstage.

Scene Nine

A huge turtle is carried in downstage right by four **Chefs** *in white hats. They put it down downstage centre and exit downstage left as* **Steevens**, **Boswell**, **Mrs Ross**, **Lord Dorset**, **Dibdin** *and* **Dr Arne** *enter upstage to gaze at it.*

Boswell   I once saw porpoises a-leaping in the Thames on a summer's day, opposite Westminster Bridge but I've never seen the like of this.

Lord Dorset   Alive it weighed three hundred and twenty-seven pounds, yet it encircled the globe, floating on warm currents like a zephyr of the deep.

Mrs Ross   This is one of the wise wanderers of the world. They navigate the Southern Seas by starlight, moonlight. Even when they've just hatched they know how to head down the sloping sand to the sunlight sea to spend their long days feeding and breeding.

Dr Arne   They live hundreds of years. This one may have swum the warm seas off the Antipodes when Shakespeare lived in England.

Dibdin   Did it ever reach these shores and see blind Lear stumble along Dover beach? Was it party to the tempest that wrecked the wicked Duke's ship?

Steevens   It must've swam in secret seas unknown to ships and men. Seas more beautiful than our lives, more transparent than our characters, where all heavens're higher, sky bluer, air fresher, moon larger, stars brighter. And in all that time it never learned meanness.

Mrs Ross   Now its long wanderings are done and its spirit rests at last, in some turtle heaven.

Lights down to the sound of pouring rain.

Scene Ten

Lights up on **Ted** *and* **Amos Ackers** *in rubber boots, laying wooden planks across the muddy stage to form cakewalks to the rotunda off stage left.*

Amos Ackers   We should get danger money for this, Ted.

Ted Ackers   They want walkways laid in time for the masquerade.

Amos Ackers   What's a masquerade?

Ted Ackers   Same as a pageant but with music and eats. They're holding it in the rotunda.

Amos Ackers   This field's a swamp.

Ted Ackers   The best Stratford sewage flows into it. Can't you smell it?

Amos Ackers   'Course I can smell it. I've never smelt a smell that smells as smelly as this smell smells. Odours rich and strange. Rabbit droppings're sweet, wild cats' stuff stinks sharp as acid drops. But beans and cabbages passing through the gut stink worse.

Ted Ackers   They say the Nuns of Eastbourne are so pure their droppings smell like soft incense on a spring morning . . . I smell yak farts in the air. We should be careful, yak gas is combustible stuff.

Amos Ackers   I dream of a god . . . not this god but another god . . . who'll blow the whole world to pieces with one single god-almighty fart.

Ted Ackers   Shakespeare never said anything as powerful as that, Amos.

Amos Ackers   How could he? He didn't know shit. He didn't know that by the age of twenty-eight every human being has produced, on their own, 30,000 tons of it. Those're facts. If Shakespeare could've talked to us he'd've learnt things about shit. We've spent our lives knee-deep in it.

They sing and dance in their rubber boots along the wooden planks.

Amos Ackers }   (*singing*) 'Stratford shifted Dad's bones
Ted Ackers }   to build a cesspit / They lifted them without a by-your-leave / They removed his remains / To lay down municipal drains / Leaving us to stand around and grieve. / That's what comes of being poor and desperate / Even after death your troubles never cease. / Just because some high priced lord / Wants a toilet for his bawd / They wouldn't let our father rest in peace.'

Lights fade down. In the half-light we see the **Guests** *for the Masquerade enter in singles or in pairs stage right or upstage. They make their way across to stage left on the wooden planks to the sound of a band playing and rain falling.*

Wheeler, **Hunt** *and* **Rev. Jago** *come on dressed as three Romans, Julius Caesar, Brutus and Antony.* **Grimes** *is Falstaff, whilst* **Steevens** *is still Prospero.* **Lydia** *as Ophelia, has a garland of daisies round her head and* **Charmaine** *as Titania has small fairy wings.* **Mrs Ross**, *in a blonde wig, is Juliet, whilst* **George Garrick** *comes as Hamlet and* **Mrs Garrick** *as Rosalind in high leather boots.* **Dibdin** *has an ass's head on as Bottom. Unfortunately so has* **Dr Arne**. *They glare at each other.* **Lord Dorset** *comes as Lear whilst* **Boswell** *is still in his Corsican outfit, but with a kilt. Lights fade to a spot on* **Garrick** *as the Chief Steward with his wand.*

Garrick   It's time for a soliloquy. But not of the old school where all is revealed to the listening air . . . (*He talks himself into a song.*) 'When misfortunes come / They are never done. / What stands on firm ground? / Everything shifts around. / You must learn to sway / Dodge and back away / Body in good trim / Stomach pulled right in / Legs steady, feet quite firm. / You are sure to learn / How not to fade / And join the Masquerade / And join the Masquerade.'

Steevens *as Prospero joins* **Garrick** *in the spot. Using his wand like a sword, he formally salutes* **Garrick**, *who formally returns the salute.*

Steevens   Time to continue the fight, sir . . .

They circle each other like duellists.

Steevens   Have a care, sir, my spittle can blind an actor for life, at twenty paces.

Garrick   Sir, as a critic you've committed every crime that doesn't require courage. It'll take a special dispensation from heaven to get you into the bottom-most pit of hell . . . defend yourself!

They fight, using their wands as swords.

Steevens   Open any Shakespeare play and what do you find?

Garrick   Words, words, words, a world of words and all different.

Steevens   You find rant, doggerel, dull jokes, crude horseplay and the deafening sound of trumpet, drum and patriotic tunes; a barbaric medley of bombast, ribaldry and blood. Is this the best our race can leave behind?

Garrick   'Once I sat upon a promontory / And heard a mermaid on a dolphin's back / Uttering such dulcet and harmonious breath, / That the rude sea grew civil at her song, / And certain stars shot madly from their spheres / To hear the sea-maid's music.' Hearing that magic, life no longer seems brief, sad and brutal.

Steevens   Or are you knowingly being bamboozled by smoke and mirrors, dazzled by Shakespeare's nimbus of renown? Are we all suffering a collective hallucination, one of those cases of national madness, like a belief in witches, the Tulip Mania or the South Sea Bubble?

Garrick   Once and only once in a nation's history comes a moment of glory, when its speech is a new-found land, when its language is molten – unhackneyed and unclichéd. It was at that moment Shakespeare appeared. With this language he created parcels of blue sky and men and women who talked themselves alive.

Steevens   No, I can't swallow his Sacred Writings whole and explain away his moral callousness . . . the bet by Posthumus about Imogen's chastity, the marriage of Celia to Oliver, of Hero to the squalid Claudio, and Isabella to the creepy Duke, the killing of poor Polonius behind the arras, the brutalisation of Kate, the approved destruction of Shylock, that vile Jew. No heavenly music, no language bright as gold can justify the moral squalor. Your

Shakespeare was a fancy pastry-cook who didn't care what
he put in his yum-yum pies so long as they sold.

Garrick   Song is the essence of human beings, all the rest
is mere conversation. Shakespeare makes his old ghosts,
squalid or not, sing. He built worlds of thought and
imagination, realms of passion and dreams which have
become places of refuge for the human spirit now and for
ever, or, at least, until this earth grows cold.

Garrick *and* **Steevens** *sink to the ground after their duel.*

Garrick   I'm exhausted, but you're wrong.

Steevens   I'm unlikeable, but I'm right.

Spot out.

Scene Eleven

Dibdin*'s 'The Warwickshire Lad' plays. Lights up on the rotunda
where the Masquerade is in progress. All the costumed* **Guests** *are
dancing whilst the rain still falls. The dancing couples talk as they
whirl past.* **George Garrick** *dances with* **Lydia***.*

Lydia   Mr Sweep, why don't you come and sweep my
chimney later?

George Garrick   Madam, the last time I swept it, I burnt
my brush. But we should talk of Shakespeare, not burning
brushes.

Lydia   I've nothing against Shakespeare but you don't
come out of any of his plays humming the tunes.

Boswell *dances past with* **Charmaine***.*

Boswell   I could've played Hamlet. I've the legs for it.
The finest pair of flashing thighs in Scotland. Even Doctor
Johnson says so, and he hates all things Scottish.

Charmaine   Wasn't Hamlet knock-kneed? And wasn't his real name Hamleth? And was it summer or winter in Elsinore when they killed each other?

Mrs Ross *dances with* **Lord Dorset**, *limping and half tripping over his long, white Lear beard.*

Mrs Ross   Did hairy Bottom get it off with Titania? An ass and a fairy, *ahhh.* I could've sold tickets for that. Jubilee prices!

Lord Dorset   Was Henry V a war criminal? Of course not. Willy S was a jingoist, through and through. He'd never show us in the wrong.

Garrick *holds up his hand.*

Garrick   Ladies and gentlemen, what you've all been waiting for . . . Signor Angelo's world-famous pyrotechnical display. In other words, the fireworks! Angelo is giving us four Tourbillons, two Figure Pieces with five vertical Wheels and spiral Wheels, twelve Chinese Jurbs, six Mortars, four dozen Water Rockets, one large Sun on top of an illuminated building with a flights of eight dozen Half-Pound Sky Rockets!

All the **Guests** *turn and look upstage. The music stops. The lights fade down, upstage. There is a pause, then the rocket is set off. It shoots up a few feet, then falls.*

Angelo's Voice   SHIT!

Garrick   That was Signor Angelo, the Italian master.

Steevens   I'm loving every minute of it. What else can happen?

Ted *and* **Amos Ackers** *rush in.*

Amos Ackers   Run for your lives, the Avon has burst its banks.

Steevens   Wonderful stuff!

Ted Ackers   It's true!

He points upstage where a great bale of blue silk unrolls. The
Guests *rush out of the rotunda and exit, stage right, as the blue silk
engulfs the whole rotunda which comes crashing down, whilst the boys'
choir is heard singing* **Arne**'s 'Thou Soft-Flowing Avon'.

Lights out.

Scene Twelve

*Sounds of panic-stricken cries in the darkness. Lights up on the muddy
field with wooden planks across it. Now the* **Guests** *are rushing away
from the rotunda along the planks, still in their costumes.*

Steevens   Critics first! A critic has to survive the debacle
so he can tell the world the scale of it.

Grimes   So you're going to blab against Master David?!

He grabs **Steevens** *and they fall off the plank into the mud,
knocking over* **George Garrick** *in the process.* **Dibdin** *and* **Dr
Arne**, *as the two Bottoms, turn on each other.*

Dr Arne   I'm the only ass here. Take off your head!

Dibdin   Take off yours, you never use it!

They fall in with a splash.

Boswell   Careful! . . . I'm getting cold mud up my kilt!

He steps on **Lord Dorset**'s *bandaged foot, who yells and they both
fall.* **Wheeler**, **Hunt** *and* **Rev. Jago** *escort* **Lydia**,
Charmaine *and* **Mrs Ross** *along a plank.*

Rev. Jago   Let me take you by the waist, ladies.

Mrs Ross   Don't forget I'm sixteen and still a virgin.

*But the plank cracks under their weight and they fall into the mud. As
the women struggle,* **Ted** *and* **Amos Ackers** *jump in to help.*

Ted Ackers ⎱
Amos Ackers ⎰ Never fear, the Ackers're here.

Garrick *and* **Mrs Garrick** *look on at the Bruegel scene with all the Shakespeare characters covered from head to foot in mud, trying to scramble off the swampy ground to dry land.* **Mrs Garrick** *moves forward to help as lights fade down to a spot on* **Garrick***. He battles against wind and rain.*

Garrick   The once proud Over-Reacher has finally over-reached himself. All's gone down. Like Agamemnon stepping out on that red carpet, I'm chopped. Aristotle would be please seeing me crushed by cold rain. It's the perfect tragic ending: hubris followed by nemesis, QED . . .

There is the sound of small bells. A line of stuffed sheep mysteriously cross upstage. It is the bells hanging round their neck that are ringing.

Garrick   Some're summoned by a word, some by a whisper, some by a sigh and some by bells. I was summoned by a dream. But it's still valid . . . Aristotle never wrote a five-acter . . . it's all theory . . . he didn't know it's only over when I say it's over. If pride brought me low then pride will save me now. I'll nail a cowpat on the roof and turn off the rain. All my life I've striven for the next prize. This one's for a dead poet. All the more reason to win. I'm alone on some dark, rainswept heath – we all come to it once in our life. We have to walk through it and the darkness and come into sunlight again. Let it piss, piss, piss down, my heart leaps up, up, up!

Spot out.

Scene Thirteen

Town Hall. The mud-covered **Guests** *are slumped shivering on chairs.* **Garrick** *enters, kisses* **Mrs Garrick***, takes off his wet jacket and rolls up his shirt sleeves as* **Mrs Garrick** *goes to the piano stage right to play a quiet accompaniment.*

Garrick   'To what blessed of the isle, / Shall gratitude her tribute pay. / To him this song and monument we raise, / He merits all our wonder, all our praise! / Yet before

impatient joy break forth / In sounds that lift the soul from
earth; / And to our spell-bound minds impart / Some faint
idea of his magic art; / With all our trumpet-tongues
proclaim, / The loved, revered, immortal name, /
SHAKESPEARE! SHAKESPEARE! SHAKESPEARE!'

The **Guests** *begin to stir and listen as an unseen chorus sings.*

Chorus (*singing*)   'Come each Muse and sister Grace /
Loves and pleasures hither come; / Well you know this
happy place, / Avon's banks were once your home. / Bring
the laurel, bring the flowers, / Songs of triumph to him
raise; / He united all your powers, / All uniting, sing his
praise!'

Garrick   'O from his muse of fire / Could but one spark
be caught, / Then might these humble strains aspire, / To
tell the wonders he has wrought . . . / When our Magician,
more inspired, / By charms and spells and incantations
fired, / Excerpts his most tremendous power; / The thunder
growls, the heavens lower, / And to his darkened throne
repair, / The demons of the deep, and spirits of the air!' . . .
(*As if on cue there is a vivid lightning bolt.*) 'But soon these horrors
pass away, / Through storms and night breaks forth the
day: / He smiles – they vanish into air!'

Chorus (*singing*)   'Wild, frantic with pleasure, / They trip
it in measure, / To bring him their treasure, / The treasure
of joy. / His rapture perceiving / They smile while they're
giving, / He smiles at receiving, / A treasure of joy.'

Garrick   'While fancy, wit and humour spread / Their
wings, and hover round his head, / And soon brought forth
a mountain of delight! / Laughter roared out to see the
sight; / And Falstaff was his name! / Wit, fancy, humour,
whim and jest, / The huge, misshapen heap impressed; /
And O – Sir John! / A comic world in one!'

Chorus (*singing*)   'Flow on, silver Avon in song ever flow, /
Be the swans on thy bosom still whiter than snow, / Ever

full by thy stream, like his fame may it spread, / And the
turf ever hallowed which pillowed his head.'

A storm breaks.

Garrick   'Nature has formed him on her noblest plan, /
And to the genius joined the feeling man. / Though with
more mortal art / Like Neptune he directs the storm, / Lets
loose like winds the passions of the heart, / To wreck the
human form.' . . . (*The storm dies down.*) 'We never shall look
upon his like again! / The song will cease, the stone decay, /
But his name / And undiminished fame, / Shall never,
never pass away.'

The grotesque mud-encased **Guests** *jump up, clapping and cheering
wildly.*

Lord Dorset   It's a wonder, sir, a wonder!

Mrs Ross   We've never heard its like.

Charmaine *and* **Lydia** *cry.*

Dr Arne   Shakespeare and the Ode're immortal!

Dibdin   The whole country will cheer.

Grimes   They'll even cheer in Glasgow.

Wheeler   Shakespeare's name will spread.

Hunt   And Stratford will grow and grow.

Rev. Jago   Give thanks to the Lord God Almighty.

Steevens   Rubbish! The Ode was as shaky as
Shakespeare's reputation. It's portentous, illogical, illiterate,
badly rhymed bombast!

George Garrick   But it works!

The others bundle **Steevens** *off.*

Boswell   This is the start of a national myth, an imperial
dream, an immortal legend. From this beginning there'll
spring a great industry. Can't you hear the machinery

turning, like the earth's slow turning in the dark? Doubters, sceptics and general nonconformists will be crushed under its unforgiving wheels and Shakespeare will bestride the coming years like a colossus. He will be as much a part of the moth-eaten tapestry of this England, as the monarchy and the Church . . . Er, could you lend me five guineas, Davey? I'm skint.

A firework display lights the darkness above them and spells out the word 'SHAKESPEARE'. That remains as the other fireworks fade and the **Guests** *exit, leaving only* **Garrick** *and* **Mrs Garrick**.

Mrs Garrick   They forgot the rain and stayed to cheer.

Garrick   An actor's triumph, short-lived as those fireworks. See how they burst and fade forever into night.

Mrs Garrick   But not 'Shakespeare'. I told you, the secret is always in the passion. And now a dead poet lights up the sky.

Lights fade out except for the word 'SHAKESPEARE' high above the stage.

Epilogue

Spot up on **Garrick** *coming downstage, wiping off his make-up.*

Garrick   On the other hand, blessed be the nameless, the good men and women whose mercy sleeps in the dark. Blessed be the warm smile and needed gesture. Blessed be the small boats passing back and forth from sea to shore. Blessed be the forgotten . . . (*The lights spelling 'SHAKESPEARE' go out.*) A fragment of melody can hold all the joy in the world. No one man has a monopoly. God listens to the shepherd playing his flute just as He listens to the poet singing his song. We are all Shakespeares! To forget that is the greatest sin of all . . . an ironmonger wanted to become a blacksmith. He bought the anvil, hammer and bellows and set to work. But nothing happened. The forge remained cold. An old man told him, 'You have everything you need except the spark. But it's easy to find, it's inside you. Just bring it out and light the forge.' . . . (*The spot begins to fade.*) . . . That's enough . . . they're turning it off and fading me out . . . it's over . . . well, don't just sit there. Go out and get a life!

Spot out.